Uniquely Qualified

Uniquely Qualified

WALK INTO YOUR DESTINY

Jacinda Jacobs

"Uniquely Qualified is captivating! Jacinda's heart jumps out from the pages of her vibrant writing, taking you on a treasure hunt of significance as you journey along your pathway to discovering your purpose...This book will awaken passion within you, as it takes you through the twists and turns of life, but connects you to a super highway that can minimize delay, while helping you avoid pitfalls as you follow your heart to bring you to your divine destination and the rarity of finding your true self."

Manny & Tracie Ohonme, Founders of Samaritan's Feet International

"We have known Jacinda for nearly six years - and she is the most caring and compassionate person we have ever met. It is unimaginable that her life was in a free fall during her teen and college years! She is constantly working for the people that have no voice or are most vulnerable. We witnessed that first hand during our health camps in India in February 2016. Physicians, nurses, and volunteers as well as patients experienced her positive and uplifting energy! Villagers and children flocked around her wherever she went. She has an uncanny ability to connect with anyone - even strangers!

She was born to serve and is "Uniquely Qualified" to do anything she chooses."

Dolly & Rakesh Agarwal of Rug and Home

Author Photography taken by Carrie Wildes Photography
Cover Design from Panagiotis Lampridis
Edited by Jean Caldwell
Scripture quotations are from *The Holy Bible.*
Charlotte, North Carolina

This is a work of nonfiction. Though the stories told in this book involve real people and actual events, some names have been changed to protect the privacy of individuals.

Printed in the United States of America.
Second Edition

ISBN: 0692814868
ISBN 13: 9780692814864

You are Uniquely Qualified.
Walk into your destiny.

Testimony shared... A destiny achieved...
Answer the Call. Take the leap.
Are you ready?

This book is dedicated to my mom. When no one else was there, you were.

TABLE OF CONTENTS

INTRODUCTION

PROVERBS 3:5

"Trust in the Lord with all your heart and
lean not on your own understanding."

Today is the day you make the change to become the person you are Uniquely Qualified to be. You are beautifully and wonderfully made, colorfully wrapped with flaws and glorious blessings. You may feel as though life's journey has taken you in a wrong direction. You have worked so hard to get to where you are, only to discover it's not what you imagined it to be. Doubt and fear begin to seep into your soul, as questions swirl through your mind. Am I worthy? What is my purpose? If I could be anything, what would I be? The answers should be simple, right?

Choose faith over fear. It was God who led you to the words on the pages that are to follow. Accept the calling that is within your current season, even if it comes with heavy burdens. Say goodbye to the comfort you built, and introduce yourself to the risks. You are Uniquely Qualified to achieve greatness. God will reveal your path. Then, it's up to you to boldly turn the knob; confidently open the door, and embrace new life.

In this book, I will share my journey of how I came to hear God awaken my heart. I was molded and put through rigorous, uncomfortable circumstances. I was brought to my knees and left hopeless. With this roller coaster ride of life, I needed to own up to my decisions. I've given thanks for my past, rather than acted as though it never happened. I am very transparent on every page. I pray you can be just as honest with yourself.

Each chapter is tailored with thought-provoking advice, activities, prayers, and blessings to equip you for your journey. Now is the time to stop fear. You are Uniquely Qualified to achieve your heart's desires. Together, we will run toward your destiny. We may even do a little dance while we're at it! Are you ready to live with extreme purpose?

> "People sooner or later discover
> that they are the master-gardener of their soul,
> the director of their life."
>
> James Allen

PREFACE

ON THE FAST TRACK

I started to smoke weed in middle school and absolutely fell in love with "the high." Smoking was my first love. I knew, no matter what, I would smoke until the day that I died. It was a part of me, and I was a part of it. Only a true smoker will understand these words. I couldn't sleep, eat, or function unless I smoked first. Then, I fell into a life of underage drinking. I began to drink and smoke daily.

My friends and I began to cut school, lie, cheat, and steal when we were only 13 years old. After only a few short years, life had already taken hold of me by the throat; suffocated the air from my lungs; and left me gasping for a way out.

Back in the day, my friends and I used to throw hotel parties. We would get older guys to get the rooms for us, since we were underage. We would go to random grocery stores. We would then steal as much alcohol that would fit into our coats and purses. We bought drugs with whatever extra money we had. I lived for the rush. My only mission was to get messed up all night long. This was the remedy I found to cure the underlying hurt I fought.

It all caught up with me when I reached the 11th grade. I was expelled from school, not for smoking, but for drinking. Go figure, the smoker got caught drinking. I got caught stumbling down the halls during a fire drill. I was completely drunk. I could barely stand up, and my classmates told on me. I was arrested on the spot, and kicked out of school. To any of my classmates reading this now, thank you, for saving my life.

At the time, I thought my life was over. I was told that I wouldn't be able to graduate, nor be allowed on school property again. I was forced to take night classes and work an 8 to 5 job. It took a probation officer and a therapist to help me get my "drug and alcohol problemed life" back together. After a year, I was allowed back on school premises and was able to walk across the stage with my class. I even managed to graduate with honors. Now, you would think I would have learned a valuable lesson, right?

I was clean for a long time, but managed to work my way back to the dark side. I looked for every chance to get high. I dated many drug dealers, just so I could get high for free. One, in particular, nearly ruined my life. Actually, I nearly ruined my life by ever dealing with him in the first place.

After a toxic relationship, a slew of misdemeanors, and losing my driver's license, my love story now faced jail time. It all started to catch up with me. I got kicked out of college shortly after that. I had no car and nowhere to live. I had no money and no self-esteem. I was 20 years old and had hit rock bottom. Is this who I'd become? How in the world did I get here? What had my life come to? I had definitely screwed up.

Ten years later, I was called to ministry. Who would have ever thought?

1

ROCK BOTTOM BLESSINGS

HEBREWS 4:12

"For the word of God is alive and powerful.
It is sharper than the sharpest two-edged
sword, cutting between soul and spirit,
between joint and marrow. It exposes our
innermost thoughts and desires."

God has always reached out for you in your life. It's whether or not you realized it that matters. You might have felt that consistent light tug, mixed with strong, uncomfortable pushes. God was always there.

You will come to know God on your own terms, in a very special way. You may have accepted God into your heart at an early age, or it may have been later in life. Regardless of that moment, it was God Who kept you safe. God has been there to guide your walk. It was God who brought you to this exact place in your life. He was, and will always be there. It was you who showed up late.

No Church Upbringing

I was not raised in the church, at all. However, it was my dad who taught me about Jesus. I believe it was important to him that he be the first person to introduce me to the concept of faith. He also explained the scientific evolution. I remember it like it was yesterday - we were living in Frankfurt, Germany. I sat with my dad as he read the encyclopedia to me. I sat in amazement as he showed pictures of an ape transitioned into human form. My dad wanted me to know both sides of how I came to be. He wanted me to find my own path.

My father was raised Catholic, so that's how my brothers and I were brought up. He taught me about the Virgin Mary; I confessed my sins and had my first Holy Communion. I went to church on holidays, which left me extremely bored. When I was a bit older, I attended Bible study on Sundays. To be honest, I never really got anything from those classes. I just went because I was forced to go. I never really made any friends and I definitely didn't learn anything.

In my adult years, my feelings changed completely, and my love for Christ flourished. It wasn't because I randomly woke up one morning and suddenly became interested in Jesus. It was because Jesus came after me. Actually, He was there all along, I just didn't realize it then. My need and undying love was birthed for Jesus after I hit rock bottom. Initially, the loss of everything in my life didn't feel good. Today, it's the best memory I hold in my heart.

TRIED SOMETHING NEW

I first started to attend church in middle school. I attended with a childhood boyfriend, Chris and his father. That was my first real church experience. After we broke up, I ventured out and tried different churches, on my own. There was a renewed curiosity that began to sprout from me.

I remember there was a big church behind my childhood home, in Hampton, Virginia. For so many years, I didn't even know it was a church. All I remember is the loud bass blasted through the walls and shook the ground all the way to our driveway. My neighbor Domi and I would run through the woods and climb trees, attempting to watch people get out of their cars and walk through the large, glass double doors into the church.

I saw tons of people gathered in the parking lot, but only on certain days. Others days of the week, the church lay dormant. I never knew what actually went on inside that building. It was like some big secret to me.

My curiosity finally brought me to that church as a teenager. I learned it was a non-denominational church. Worship was like nothing I had ever experienced before. People of all ages, young and old, clapped their hands and praised. There was a mix of culture, from white and black, to Hispanic and Asian. Everyone jumped around, and some cried. It didn't matter if you were filthy rich, or poor, this church was inclusive to all walks of people. It was beautiful.

I witnessed a woman cry and scream all at the same time. I believe she was overwhelmed with the joy of the Holy Spirit, but at the time, I can't lie to you, it scared me. I saw another family grab flags, and run with them down the aisles. I had no idea what that meant. I felt completely uncomfortable. I sat alone, in silence. I had never experienced anything like this in my life. Up until that point, I had never even clapped in church. All the excitement had me intrigued. I wondered if I could ever be that happy and full of life, like them.

One Man's Persistence

Fast forward to my college years. After I hit the lowest of the low, I was at rock bottom. I didn't have a car. I lost all my money. I got kicked out of college, had no job, and faced serious criminal charges. I was in desperate need of a second chance at life.

Within a couple weeks, I met a wonderful woman who gave me an opportunity to waitress at Olive Garden. I worked day and night, to make ends meet. This job allowed me to get back on my feet. To this day, Olive Garden still holds a special place in my heart. It was over breadsticks and salad that I experienced a defining moment that changed my life, forever.

There was a Pastor who frequented Olive Garden with his family. Pastor Ron would request to sit in my section every time. As I served him, he would always talk to me and inquire about my life. It was difficult to share such dark stories with a stranger, let alone a Pastor. It became difficult to serve other tables while he was there due to his long list of questions. With his persistence, I started to unfold the broken pieces of my life. I shared my testimony of drug and alcohol abuse, and dead-end relationships. I confessed everything to him raw and uncut.

I was a 21-year-old girl. All I wanted to do was make it in the world, but I had ruined any chance of it. To make matters more difficult, my mom worked and lived in Barbados, and my father was no longer in our lives. I was the legal guardian of my two younger brothers. My personal life was also in shambles, as I faced an enormous amount of trouble with the law. I guess Pastor Ron thought the best way to help this poor girl was to bring her to his church. He invited me every chance he got. I graciously declined, each time. I was grateful for his invitation, but I just didn't want to go. I had given up.

For a couple of months, I managed to duck and dodge Pastor Ron's continued efforts. However, as I told you earlier, he was extremely persistent. Pastor Ron knew exactly when I worked and popped up weekly. It made me feel like he was there for more than just a meal. I had become his mission. There was no getting around him. I eventually ran out of excuses and reluctantly decided to take him up on his offer. I figured if I went at least one time, he would finally leave me alone.

You can only run for so long when God is calling you. It's like a constant nagging tug that won't go away. Guess what? God will always win.

Some of us have slight difficulties when it comes to trust, especially, if it's a stranger. We begin to think the person is nosey or will judge us. Pray and ask God who you should share your life with. Remember, we are not meant to do life alone. God will always place people in your life to help you. If you stay closed off forever, how can someone else pull you out of your darkness?

Found Salvation

Pastor Ron's church was small and intimate. I loved his energy as he preached the Word of God. His passion made me feel like it wasn't just empty, dead-end words anymore. When it came time for salvation, I felt something shoot right through me. God called me to Him. I was too embarrassed to take that walk in front of everyone. God pushed me to stand up, but I could barely feel my legs, I was so scared. Actually, I was terrified. My knees felt like they were about to give out at any second, I shook uncontrollably as sweat began to roll down my face. I wanted to burst into tears and scream at the top of my lungs, all at the same time.

My face was bright red. I sobbed as God told me the time was now. I had tried every other option on my own. Those decisions left me broken, with absolutely nothing to show, other than painful memories. This time, I was ready to surrender to something more powerful than myself.

On that day, at Pastor Ron's church, I finally answered the call and raised my hand. Pastor Ron walked over and asked me to join him up front. I braced myself for what was to come next. Low and behold, he started to tell my story, in front of everyone in the congregation. He shared how I was all alone, with my brothers, and that I had messed up so many times. Then, he said the most beautiful words, "God loves you," as he stretched out his hand for mine, he added, "The victory has already been won." I felt my back stiffen as I stood tall. As he told my story, I was no longer ashamed. I realized, for the first time in my life, God had something great in store for me. I came with a lot of baggage, but on that day, my baggage seemed lighter. The heavy weight I carried on my shoulders was lifted. I was saved!

Being saved was just the first step. The temptations of my past were still present. In some cases, they were even stronger. However, for the first time in my life, I knew God was in my midst.

"When you hold onto your history,
you do it at the expense of your destiny."

Bishop T.D. Jakes

P.S.

When you first get saved, don't expect to see a complete transformation, instantly. Don't expect yourself to be perfect. No perfect person even exists. A true transformation takes time and spiritual growth. It's a faith journey you have the privilege to take for the rest of your life, a daily walk. There will still be high mountains to climb and deep valleys to cross. Take one step at a time and never quit. Your consistency in this walk is the key to unlock the destination God has designed perfectly for you.

The Bible is Your BFF

My best friend Nay and her mom, Ms. Gloria showered me with two very, special gifts at my college graduation. You read that right! Yes, I eventually got back into school and yep, even graduated. One of the gifts they got me was a lily plant.

The card attached to it read, "May this plant grow with your success." Needless to say, every move I ever made, whether it was to another state or simply into a new apartment, this plant sat in my passenger seat with the seatbelt on. The second gift was the New Living Translation Bible. Up until this point, the only Bible I ever saw was the one in hotel rooms that sat in the desk drawers. Thank you Ms. Gloria for saving me. She showed me that there was an easier way to read and understand the Bible. In the NLT version, I was finally able to appreciate the powerful messages behind each story. What began as complicated words in biblical times, now had become stories I could apply to my life. Word by word, I started to fall in love with Jesus. I began to experience Him in a real and passionate way. He was no longer just a man preachers talked about on Sundays. With a turn of every page, I found myself wanting more.

When you love someone, you want to be with them. You want to see them constantly, and spend as much time with them as possible. This is all God asks of you. He wants you to be near Him. Not because you have to, but simply, because you want to.

It perplexes me how most of us have never read the Bible completely. We sit for hours at a time to watch a movie. It may take days or weeks to finish a good book. Some of us even binge watch our favorite television series. However, only a small number of people have taken the time to read the Bible. The Bible is our blueprint for life. Why isn't this the first book we're taught to read? The stories, people, and underlined messages all provide answers to life's questions and uncertainties. Don't run from the Bible, run toward it. Allow the Bible to be your road map for life.

SAY YES TO GOD

If you haven't accepted Jesus Christ as your Lord and Savior, or if you would like to rededicate your life to Christ, read this prayer to yourself now. It's not the prayer that saves you, it's what you believe in your heart.

"Dear God in Heaven, I come to You in the name of Jesus. I acknowledge to You that I am a sinner, and I am sorry for my sins and the life that I have lived I need Your forgiveness.

I believe that Your only begotten Son Jesus Christ shed His precious blood on the cross at Calvary. He died for my sins. I am now willing to turn from my sins.

You said in Your Holy Word, Romans 10:9: "If we confess the Lord our God and believe in our hearts that God raised Jesus from the dead, we shall be saved."

Right now, I confess Jesus as the Lord of my soul. With my heart, I believe that God raised Jesus from the dead. This very moment, I accept Jesus Christ as my own personal Savior; and according to His Word, right now I am saved.

Thank You, Jesus, for dying for me and giving me eternal life. AMEN."

Never forget this moment.

Date: ______________________

Time: ______________________

2

DISCOVER YOUR GIFT

EPHESIANS 2:1-5

"And you were dead in your trespasses and sins, in which you formerly walked according to the course of this world, according to the prince of the power of the air, of the spirit that is now working in the sons of disobedience. Among them we too all formerly lived in the lusts of our flesh, indulging the desires of the flesh and of the mind, and were by nature children of wrath, even as the rest. But God, being rich in mercy, because of His great love with which He loved us, even when we were dead in our transgressions, made us alive together with Christ (by grace you have been saved)."

Deep down, we all desire to be loved and accepted by others. But, many of us cross the line and become more of what I like to call, "attention seekers." Here's a quick test to determine if this is you or not. When you take a group picture with friends, do you immediately look for yourself in the photo, or do you look at your friends first? If you answered truthfully, you probably said, yourself. In all honesty, you probably didn't even notice anyone else in the picture for the first few seconds. Now let's use social media for next test. When it comes to your Facebook, Twitter, Instagram and Snap Chat accounts, do you check to see how many "likes" and "views" you've generated? Do you compare your numbers to your friends? Most of us have fallen victim to the "like" button and I am no different.

My hunger for attention started at a very young age. I wanted to be "liked" so badly. I wanted my friends to like me, I wanted boys to like me. We didn't have social media back then, so there wasn't a "like" button anyone could click to make me feel a sense of worth. I found my fame when I smoked and drank. I fit in when I cursed and stole from the store with my friends. I was popular when I slept around and skipped class. Shoot, I was on my way to real stardom! Little did I know, God had prepared a different kind of "spotlight" for me. One that didn't consist of drugs and sex like I thought I wanted. God had greater plans in store for me.

Be careful not to get consumed in your search for love and acceptance. It will only leave you broken and empty. That unwavering love you are in search for can only be found in Jesus.

Front and Center

In high school God gave me the unique quality of public speaking. When it was time for class presentations, I always volunteered to go first. Most of my classmates were too scared to go second or even third, for that matter. I take that back; they never wanted to present at all. That was the difference between me and them. I was excited to stand in front, while they watched and listened as I spoke. Presenting came natural to me, it was gratifying. That was when I noticed I was different.

I joined the Forensics Speech and Debate Team, and used it to practice delivery of speeches. One day, I showed up to class and had completely forgotten that I had a presentation. As I walked to my seat, I was excited to present; but I knew nothing about the subject matter. This brought on a sense of uneasiness. I gathered some quick research and put my thoughts in order. As soon as class started, I raised my hand and informed the teacher that I was ready to present. With overwhelming confidence, I walked to the front of the class and stared each person in their eyes. I grabbed everyone's attention with the use of my dramatic pauses. Expert speakers use these types of techniques as attention grabbers. They are also used to slow down the pace and establish control over the presentation and audience. I observed, as my classmates responded uncomfortably to those pauses. They probably thought I had messed up or had gotten nervous. That wasn't the case, at all. I, the presenter, had demanded their attention. All eyes were on me. My classmates clung to my every word. They ate out the palm of my hand and I loved every second of it. On that day, as I stood in front of that classroom, my gift was born. I was unprepared and put on the spot, but my gift outshined it all. I received an A+ on that presentation.

Do you know your gifts and talents? If you do, take a moment to reflect on the time your gift was revealed to you.

Be keenly aware of these defining moments in your life. Once you come face-to-face with your talent, it becomes your job to develop it. In order to move forward in this journey, you have to reflect a bit. One of the best moments in your life is when God gives you a glimpse of your purpose.

If you are unsure of your abilities, just ask yourself what is the thing you love to do that doesn't feel like work. Everyone has a set of abilities that they excel in. Prime example: My girlfriend Tyler loves to watch TV. To be more specific, she mainly loves sitcoms. Tyler can watch these shows repeatedly. You may look at this as a problem, but I see it as a disguise for true purpose.

There have been times I have invited her to go out with me, but she refused to go because her favorite show was on. In fact, she was hired to tweet about the show. If you are someone who is unsure of your gifts, talents, and abilities, here's a cool way to figure it out. Identify your interests.

Tyler's interest in sitcoms led her to look into the development of her own. There are teams of people who work in the background to conceptualize ideas and storylines. These thoughts turn to scripts, then transition into episodes. It's awesome, creative people like this can bring film, TV shows and plays to life. Then, boom you have a hit! If you think about it for a second, that's exactly what God does. God works behind the scenes to develop your gifts. He creates your script, develops your movie, reveals the climax, then drum roll please, your purpose is revealed.

Today, my friend Tyler has created her own screenplay. She's on different TV show and movie sets weekly. She even got to meet Oprah in 2016! Tyler hopes to become a scriptwriter and director for a feature film, in the near future. So, before you can see the finished project, I ask you again, what do you love? What fuels your heart with passion? What are your interests? What can you not live without? What would you love to wake up and do every day?

Magic in the Mic

Thanks to all the good tips I saved up from Olive Garden, I eventually got back on my feet. I even picked up a part-time job on a dinner cruise liner, called the Spirit of Norfolk.

As a server, I would shine silverware, set the tables, serve food and drinks, and entertain. I couldn't believe my job description required that I sing and dance with all my guests. I still don't know how I managed to work this job, due to my horrible motion sickness. To this day, I can't even ride in the passenger seat of a car without a constant battle with nausea.

Yet, there I was on that boat, every day. I thoroughly enjoyed my job, except when I really had to work. By work, I mean, when everyone had fun, I'd have to carry these huge trays of dirty dishes down the stairs to the kitchen. Then, once everyone left, I had to lug those now cleaned dishes back up the stairs to set up for the next cruise.

Over time, the tray on my shoulder grew heavier, as my attention turned toward DJ Madd Mixx. I no longer wanted to be a server. Instead, I wanted his job. I wanted to be the fun person who hyped the crowd. There was something about that mic that called my name, and I wanted it!

I became close friends with DJ Madd Mixx. It just so happened he was an on-air personality for one of the major top 40 radio stations, in Virginia Beach, Virginia. One day, he invited me into the radio station for a tour. I needed an internship and, since I'd majored in Communications, it was perfect. I was immediately blown away.

The station included an air hockey table and flashing fluorescent lights. The latest tunes blasted through the loudspeakers. It was the coolest atmosphere I had ever seen. It was like out of a movie. The account execs rocked stylish clothes, joked, laughed, and had so much fun. I couldn't believe this was a real work environment.

I always envisioned my future career in a dark office, with no windows. An environment as cool as this radio station was never in my radar, but I loved every second of it. DJ Madd Mixx introduced me to Zach Daniels, from the Freak Show. He had his own evening slot and, surprisingly, needed an intern. The magic of the mic shifted my life, and my "On-Air" light switched on. My transition had begun.

Captain Planet

Life has a funny way of working out sometimes, doesn't it? In high school, I developed a passion for public speaking. However, a few years prior, I'd wanted to be an environmental engineer. All I'd wanted to do was save the planet. How in the world could my interests jump from two completely different career fields? I remember my best friend Adrienne and I would stop by an ice cream truck, after school. I absolutely loved those strawberry shortcake ice cream bars.

On that particular day, as we walked home, she threw her ice cream wrapper on the ground. I said to myself, "Oh no she didn't." I was so passionate about the cleanliness of the environment, I asked her to pick up her trash. I could not believe my friend tried to contribute to pollution. With attitude and anger, she obliged. This memory still makes us laugh.

Did you really think you would be where you are today? Calculate all the crossroads and decisions you've made that have gotten you to this point. The best part is, you can change your tomorrow, today.

If your heart screams for more, consider the relationships in your life. It's important to reflect on the people who have come into your life. People within your circle, and even strangers may shape and propel you into the path of your destiny. Your next step could be tied to a handshake or a hug.

Just as Pastor Ron led me to salvation, DJ Madd Mixx connected me to radio. Say "yes" as you meet people, and say "yes" to new possibilities. You could be one handshake away from your destiny.

YOUR I AM'S

Words are powerful. They speak life or death over you. Think about the small catch phrases you say daily. You may not realize just how much you have doomed your future, based on what you say. For instance, someone may ask you how you are. You may respond with, "Just trying to make it." Unconsciously, you have just given power to that statement and declared a mentality of struggle. You can change your circumstances based on the words that come out of your mouth. Why not answer with a reply like: "I am amazing." "I am blessed to be alive." "I am grateful to be here another day." "I am so happy to see you." Now, you have spoken life over yourself.

It's time to develop your I Am statement. It's one of the most important statements that will come out of your mouth. Be careful what you say, after "I am." It will ring true in your life. If you say, "I am broke," then you just spoke financial hardship over your life. When you jokingly follow with words like, "I am unhappy, lost, angry, fat, lonely, etc.," you have spoken these things into existence. Know and learn your I Am statement. Post it on your mirror and speak it, daily. Why were you created? What is the destiny God has designed for you? Your I Am statement should reflect these answers.

Jacinda's "I Am" Statement:
I Am a Servant for Jesus Christ.

Now, it's time for you to write your "I Am" Statement:

____

____

____

3

WALK INTO YOUR SEASON

Ecclesiastes 3:1-8

"To every thing there is a season, and a time to every purpose under the heaven: A time to be born, and a time to die; a time to plant, and a time to pluck up that which is planted; a time to kill, and a time to heal; a time to break down, and a time to build up; a time to weep, and a time to laugh; a time to mourn, and a time to dance; a time to cast away stones, and a time to gather stones together; a time to embrace, and a time to refrain from embracing; a time to get, and a time to lose; a time to keep, and a time to cast away; a time to rend, and a time to sew; a time to keep silence, and a time to speak; a time to love, and a time to hate; a time of war, and a time of peace."

On my first day as an intern, I thought I would copy papers and bring coffee. Nope. Zach Daniels handed me a pair of headphones; sat me in front of the mic, and said: "Laugh when I point to you." This idea was to make listeners think the studio was packed with people. Fast forward a few months, and we were a dynamic duo on the airwaves. My on-air personality was a saucy, sassy, firecracker chick that never agreed with anyone. I could not believe people enjoyed my personality.

I used slang words because, at the time, I cursed like a sailor and didn't have what I believe was the intelligence to use correct grammar. Little did I know, I walked into a natural ability of entertainment.

Lucky for me, a new Program Director came and took over the station. Michael Bryan had listened to us for weeks, prior to his arrival. He was intrigued by my talent, and hired me as soon as my internship ended. He gave me my very own show, on the weekend. I couldn't believe I worked at the coolest place in America.

As a hungry student in my craft, I tested out different on-air formats, like Top 40, R&B, Talk Radio and Hot Adult Contemporary, which ultimately became my favorite. I read local news updates for syndicated shows, like the Steve Harvey Morning Show and Wake Up with Whoopi. I also became a Traffic Reporter for surrounding stations, and used the fake name, Lacy Shay.

These moments defined my first three years in the radio business. While my friends ran around town and let loose at college parties, little did I know, I had launched my career.

Once I graduated, I eagerly awaited my first promotion. I fully expected to move up from part-time work, to a full-time slot, with benefits. Not only did I have the experience, I now had the degree to back it up. I had that where-do-I-sign attitude.

I went to John, the General Manager to let him know that I was interested in joining the team on a fulltime basis. I had worked nearly every role at the station. I developed a reputation as the "go-to girl." He eagerly told me, "Yes ma'am, we love you and want you here." That quick "yes" was followed with a stipulation. He smiled and informed me of his plans to move me into a full-time, on-air role. But, he told me I would have to wait three months. My excitement and hurried momentum, were put on pause.

God will slow you down, from time to time. There's a reason for that. We serve a God Who knows us better than we know ourselves. Each time you are forced to wait, God will reveal circumstances to you and show your strength. How bad do you want it? You want it now, don't you? It may take days, weeks, or even years. Your extreme patience will determine your spiritual maturity. Wait on God's perfect timing.

Smack You in the Face

You can never truly imagine how cool it is to work at a radio station, unless you've experienced it for yourself. One afternoon, a high school class took a tour of the station. The students and their teachers crowded around one the sound board, in the studio. One student asked Christy, the afternoon personality if she knew the function of all the buttons. I remember Christy specifically tell the students she only knew how to work a few. She had no idea what the other buttons were for.

I had worked so hard at the station; I knew what every button did. Shoot, I used most of them. I never said anything to her or ruined the moment for the students, but that was a reality check for me. Christy was a talented woman, who got paid good money to work the perfect schedule. Yet, she didn't know how to run the board. I did, however, but was still considered a part-time employee. This was a breakthrough moment in my life, where I realized I was not fairly compensated for my work, talent, or time.

The Jump

Three months quickly came and went. To my shock and amazement, John never promoted me, as he'd promised. I was like a kid in the candy store, being told by my mother not to touch the sweet candy of my dreams. I waited eagerly for the next movement in my career to take place, but it never happened. The station simply moved around current, full-time employees to justify job obligations. I remained a part-time, on-air personality. I learned a valuable lesson. I could not sit and wait on someone to deliver my big break. I had to go get it. I quit.

What risks are you willing to take to get what you want out of life? There are times when you may be forced to jump off a cliff. Will you take that leap of faith? Others may call you crazy, but I want to prepare you for the jump, as well as share what happens afterwards. That's what you'll learn in this book. I urge you to think long and hard about your destiny. You need the faith and the confidence in God to take that first step. Many people will come to this four-way intersection, but fear will stop them. However, you are Uniquely Qualified to step into the unknown. Your faith, hard work, and obedience will connect you to your destiny.

What's Your Mission Statement?

Let's write a mission statement for your life. Many of us have an objective statement on our resume. We've written down our dreams in our journals and attended vision board parties. What about you and God? What is God's plan for you? Let's speak to your internal Holy Spirit for this exercise.

This mission statement will give you a goal to live for. It will be the road map you take onto the path of your destiny. This is a dark exercise, as we typically don't want to think about what happens after we're dead and gone. But, bear with me.

A friend, Cyril Prabhu, taught me this mission statement exercise. It's called, "The Toast." It makes you reflect on your life; take deep regard for the person you are right now; as well as focus on the person you wish to become. You are a constant work in progress. So, why not make bold changes in your life, now? I believe everyone should do this exercise in their adult life.

Let's dive in. Think about the day you leave this Earth. You have passed away. Family and close friends have come to your funeral. Immediately afterwards, everyone gathers for food, drinks, and conversation. Imagine all your family and friends, assembled around the table. Each one gives a toast in your honor. Consider who will be there to speak love and legacy over your life. Your first step in this activity is to list at least 10 people who will present a toast to your name.

The next step is to write down what each person will say in their toast. Consider the stories they will share. Reminisce on the memories they hold near and dear. The key to this activity is to envision what you would like each person so say about you.

What did they like about you? How were you a good friend? What things did you do for them that no one else ever did? How is their life impacted now that you're gone? Take your time as you write down their answers. If you cry and/or take a long time on this step, it's okay. This is heavy, as it may bring up a lot of memories and emotions. However, it is one of the most important exercises you will ever do.

Once your page is filled up, read over each toast. Ask yourself if you are truly the person they've referenced. Do you like what you see on this piece of paper? Did you struggle to come up with good things to say? It's important for you to understand how your loved ones perceive you. Be aware and acknowledge who you are and how you impact others. If you do not like what people may say, the change starts now. Become the person you are truly destined to be; the person others will fall in love with.

For the last step, circle all the verbs on the page and write them down underneath your list. For example, circle words like, loving, caring, listens, etc. Use these words to develop your mission statement. This mission statement will represent an objective to live toward in your life. It's important for you to think about your legacy and what you want to leave behind. The goal is to create a mission statement for your life that will leave an imprint of worth, every step you take. Start now.

Step 1. List 10 names of people who will give a toast and write out their toast to you.

____

____

____

____

____

____

____

____

____

____

Step 2. Circle all the verbs from each toast.

Step 3. Create your official Mission Statement.

____

____

____

____

____

____

____

____

____

____

Jacinda's mission statement:
"My Mission is to be a Strong, Loving, Loyal, Teaching, Bold, Woman of God"

4

IT'S TIME TO FLY

John 16:33

"I have told you these things, so that in
Me you may have peace. In this world,
you will have trouble. But take heart!
I have overcome the world."

Without a backup plan, I created one out of thin air. I started to plan a move back to my hometown of Miami, Florida. My goal was to go back to school to get a master's degree. I would pick up a small job to make ends meet. I found a townhome and began to pack up my place in Virginia. In the meantime, I continued to apply for radio jobs, but found nothing. Then, the phone rang and it changed everything.

The Queen City

A fairly new Top 40 radio station opened up in Charlotte, NC. They were interested in hiring me as a morning show co-host and producer. I jumped in my car and went for an impromptu interview. The gig seemed to be the job of a lifetime. The co-hosts were cool, and the money was great. The role would launch me into some sort-of local celebrity in Charlotte.

I was intrigued. They called and offered the job as I stood in line to rent a truck for my move to Miami. In that instance, I risked it all. I jumped out of line; cancelled the townhome rental in FL, and broke up with my then boyfriend. I loaded up my car and, in only four days, I hit I-85 South, as I sung my theme song for this new journey, "Big Girls Don't Cry," by Fergie.

At this point in my life, I didn't know what it meant to pray daily. I only prayed when I really needed something, as most of us tend to do. I was familiar with God, but He was not my foundation yet. As I recall this story, I laugh at how God had orchestrated my steps for His glory. He worked out all the pieces behind the scenes but I couldn't even see it.

It was all a part of God's plan. Whether we know God or not, He's always walked ahead of us and prepared the journey. He walks before us, carries us, and stays alongside us, all at the same time.

Think back to your yesterdays. God has worked everything out for you this entire time. He has gently glided you into this path toward your destiny. Moments of reflection allow for you to see your progression, and to give thanks to God as He moves behind the scenes. Know that He was there whether you knew it or not. He has always been there. Thank Him, right now.

Jacinda with the Sleazy

I worked as a co-host and producer for a major market radio show, Brotha Fred's AM Mayhem with David L, Jacinda, and Cubby - and, what a freaking, awesome job it was! I would get up at 3am to arrive at the station to prepare for our 6am show. I would talk junk, laugh, and dish out the "sleazy," which was my celebrity gossip and entertainment segment.

The best part for me was, I got to drink coffee every morning and got to clown with my co-hosts and listeners. It was so much fun! I couldn't believe this was actually my job. I had my first grown-up job, and it didn't even feel like work. Had I stayed in Virginia, and waited on that full-time, on-air position to open up, I may have never experienced a career move of this magnitude.

To land a job like this, right out of college, is almost unheard of. I was on my own, as I explored a new city and a new life. I attended many social events and concerts. As a child, I did not attend any professional sports games. So, I took advantage and attended all sports related activities, such as basketball, football, baseball, hockey, and NASCAR. I engulfed myself in the single, young-professional lifestyle. I took a nosedive into the city of Charlotte. I mean, it was a head first, eyes closed, beautiful form type of dive.

When the door of opportunity opens, don't walk through it; run! Life tends to be a waiting game. Do not hesitate to take the first step to experience a breakthrough. You may worry about what lies ahead, when a season of blessings showers upon you. You may even say, "Oh, something bad has to happen soon, because life has been so great." Relax. Bask in the greatness that you so deserve. Remember to enjoy life.

Soar Higher

Have you ever experienced a moment in your life when your reality became bigger than your dream? Wow! I challenge you to close your eyes and envision your dream. Now, think bigger than that dream. Don't get scared, anxious, or timid about what is to come. God has big plans for you.

Jeremiah 29:11 says, "For I know the plans I have for you," says the Lord, "They are plans for good and not for disaster, to give you a future and a hope." That's what God wants for your future, for you to have hope and prosperity. Open yourself up to the possibility that you can and will soar high beyond the clouds.

Living the Good Life

I feel like Charlotte welcomed me with opened arms. There was one prayer I said repeatedly. Remember, I was not a person who knew how to pray. For some reason, however, I continuously prayed for God to bring good people into my life. I was young, alone, in a new city, and away from family and friends. I prayed for God to send people into my life who would protect, care for, teach, and open me up to new possibilities. I met some of the greatest people a girl could ever ask for.

The move to Charlotte wasn't just a career move to me.

It was a new beginning; a second chance; and what I call, "a pivotal moment in my life." I had to take responsibility for my past decisions, party lifestyle, and bad choices. With my move to a new city, if those situations had followed me, it would have been no one's fault but my own. I no longer had anyone to blame. As I embarked on a new life, I made a personal commitment to eliminate any self-inflicted drama. Thank You, God. You saved me from me.

I believe there are two types of situations that happen in life. First, there are situations you cause yourself. It's called, "cause and effect." The result in these situations are due to something you did or did not do. For example, if you are repeatedly tardy to work, this will eventually lead to termination. Or, failure to pay the mortgage will end with eviction. Then, there are situations you cannot escape in this thing called life. This is when life serves you a dose of its best drawbacks.

Imagine you are on your way to work on a Monday morning. You got up early; left the house on time; but, there's more traffic than normal. As you put on your blinker and merge into your left lane, a car smashes into the back of your car. This, my friend, is life. These types of situations are uncontrollable, unknown pop-ups that you cannot run from. There is nothing you can do with these circumstances of life, other than face them.

However, out of both types of situations, you can only prevent the ones you cause yourself. So, why not try and make life a little easier on yourself? You have the right and the power, to determine a piece of your future.

Matthew 6: 33-34

"But seek first the Kingdom of God and His righteousness and all these things shall be added to you. Therefore, do not worry about tomorrow for tomorrow will worry about its own thing. Sufficient for the day is its own trouble."

WAKE UP WITH GOD

Psalm 29:11

"The Lord gives His people strength.
The Lord blesses them with peace."

Set devotional time with God. There's power in the stillness of the Lord, but, you must slow your life down in order to receive it. To begin devotional time, consider how your mornings start now. What was the first thing you did once you hit the alarm clock today? Did you rush through your morning routine? Did you jump on your cell phone and check emails? Did you view your social media?

The way your day unfolds has a lot to do with how you started it. You put your mind through brain overload of meaningless, endless thoughts, first thing in the morning. This is why you feel overwhelmed, by lunch time. Before you even walked out the door, you oversaturated your mind with news, entertainment, and the thoughts of, "I'm going to be late."

Some people cry about how early they wake up, already. They complain. They say they don't have time, in their busy schedule, to just simply pray to God. Make no excuses for not completing this activity. Consider what you are asking God to do in your life. When you ask God to do the impossible in your life, then you must learn to bask in His presence.

The first step is to spend devotional time with God. Set an alarm to wake up a few minutes earlier, maybe even an hour earlier. If you are a person who revolves around a calendar schedule, then schedule devotional time with God, if need be. Take baby steps, initially. Do not touch your phone, or log online first thing in the morning. Do not wake up your kids, first.

This is your alone time with God. Pour your heart out to God and share your gratefulness. Over time, you will be filled with excitement to wake up with God. You will notice the length of your devotional time with God will increase. You will also observe a shift in the way you feel, during the day.

It's hard to explain, but spending time with God first thing in the morning, is a time to cover yourself in His love and guidance. It's as if you put on a suit of armor, of God's grace and mercy. You may have a million tasks to do that day, but watch as God allows you to accomplish more in less time. Your perspective will change as you become more in line with God's will for your life.

Here are some ideas that will help grow your devotional time. First, purchase a devotional book filled with small prayers and scriptures. You may want to put it on your nightstand. Over time, you may find your nightstand filled with your Bible, devotionals, inspirational books, and journals. Other ideas include download prayer apps; watch your favorite preachers share great, empowering messages; watch Bible studies and listen to uplifting music, as you get dressed.

Any of these suggestions set a positive tone for the day that lies ahead. Develop a strong morning ritual, to feed your soul. This time with God is a weapon against the enemy. It's your ammunition.

5

FAITH CHANGES THINGS, LITERALLY

JAMES 1:6

"But let Him ask in faith, nothing wavering.
For He that wavers is like a wave of the
sea driven with the wind and tossed."

Once I got settled in at the radio station, one of the first things I did was go "church shopping." This is when you search for a church to call your home. After I visited five churches, my co-host David L recommended that I try Nations Ford Community Church. I checked it out the very next Sunday, and immediately fell in love.

I was greeted with warm hugs and smiles as I walked through the doors. I felt welcomed and loved. Every person I met genuinely invested themselves into my faith journey. This meant the world to me. You see, this church is a predominately African American church and I come from two different cultures. My father is from the Dominican Republic and my mom is a white American.

In a heavily, racially, driven society, you would expect a congregation to be shocked that a woman like myself just walked through the double doors. That was never the case at Nations Ford. They all welcomed me. The loved me and I'll never forget it. From random church attendance as a child, to curiosity-driven church visitations as a young adult, I had finally found my first church home. I joined and began to serve.

It's important for you to have a church home for your spirit to grow. You are not meant to go through life alone. You need a home church to help you get connected to other believers. You need people to pick you up when you're down and strengthen you when you're weak, and to pray for you when you can't pray for yourself. It doesn't matter how much TV you watch to receive an inspirational word. In this life, you need people who you can walk alongside for support.

Your spirit will immediately let you know when you've found your church home. You will experience an overwhelming sensation of ultimate peace. Sometimes, this awareness happens before you even realize it. It doesn't matter how small, or how large the church is; it's God plan for your spirit to grow there and be connected with others who are on the same journey. Every tree must be planted deep into the soil to grow strong. Just as a tree has roots, you should too.

The church is your foundation, your soil for spiritual growth. In Psalm 1:3 it says, "They are like trees planted along riverbanks, bearing fruit each season. Their leave never wither, and they prosper in all they do." Don't force yourself to find the perfect church home, immediately. Allow God to lead you to it. This process takes time.

All Cursed Out

After I joined the church, I decided to get baptized. I wanted to make the choice myself, as an adult. I wanted God to know that I was ready to leave my past behind me. For some strange reason, with this new chapter, my spirit constantly urged me to give something up. There were certain things I was not ready to give up. However, I was ready to clean up my potty mouth. It was pretty vulgar. My life was f@&! this and motha-f@&! that.

My former radio co-host would laugh and say he could taste the words coming out of my mouth, because I projected them with such aggression. I had a rough exterior that didn't put up with any mess. I was one tough chick. It was at this point that I learned I only, boastfully, spoke my own insecurities.

After my baptism, I took a huge step and fell in line with God's plan for my life. I truly desired to become a lady. I wanted to be a woman that young ladies could look up to. Yet, I displayed no image of this lady.

I challenged myself to come up with other words to use, instead of profanity, that would still deliver the same emotion. I no longer allowed my ignorance to shine. I made the choice to showcase my worth. I was educated. I was beautiful. I was, and still am, a profound woman who young girls look up to.

I thank God for His guidance, which gave me the strength. I successfully accomplished this feat and stopped cursing. Then, rolled a blunt to celebrate. How ironic was that? I asked God to clean up my foul language, yet had no intentions to quit smoking. I still wanted to get high. I used to tell myself I would never quit.

As I turned my cheek, I asked God to only have His hand on particular areas of my life that I wanted to fix. There were other parts of me that I did not want God to touch. But, I couldn't be the boss of God. I would tell Him, "I got this over here, I don't need Your help." I would be forced to face it, eventually. I belittled God's grace every time I held onto things that were bad. Why should God bless me? I wasn't even ready to receive it.

Empty Substance

I loved my new church family. This foundation strengthened my faith walk, tremendously. I was appreciative of the positive strides that had begun to shape my life. However, I didn't think they would take a negative toll on my job. I started to battle with my on-air, judgmental comments. It became hard for me to push the envelope with risqué chatter. I could no longer bring myself to talk about who I'd had sex with, or who I wanted to have sex with.

Yes, that was our morning banter. Even though they were all jokes, I felt a level of responsibility. I started to feel like I had no substance. What did God think? I grew empty inside. All I had were meaningless jokes, with tons of listeners who held onto every word.

My work in the public eye made me vulnerable. Some mornings, I would cry nonstop, because I felt I could no longer portray this woman of low standards. I felt as though I had abandoned my co-hosts and compromised my faith□ all at the same time. Here I was at, yet, another crossroad in life. I thought this job would fix everything, but it was only a temporary Band-Aid on a huge scar. I learned it had nothing to do with the job, and everything to do with God.

When you transition from a life without God, to one of prayer and faith, you will be challenged. You will feel the pull and it will be uncomfortable. You will want to take the step, but questions of uncertainty will arise. How can you walk away from everything you know and love? How do you know if you will like this new world of faith?

You may go through mental exhaustion and your emotions will be in a whirlwind. You may be all alone, with no friends, and no one to understand you. But just know, once you make the choice to walk toward your faith in God, you will walk into an abundance of everything you have ever prayed for.

Congrats, You're Fired

Rather than make the difficult choice myself, the station did it for me. One Friday afternoon, I was let go from the morning show. They said the station was "headed in a different direction." I was grateful to be free. Two of my best friends came into town that weekend from Virginia, so I turned it into a celebration. I tried to embrace the closed door. I kept a big smile on my face and remained positive. But, in all honesty, I shook and trembled inside. I had no idea what to do next.

Public embarrassment added another difficult layer to my

break up with the station. I had connected with so many listeners. Over three years, we had all become part of each other's morning routines. Two things hit me on that Sunday evening. First, I didn't have to wake up at 3am.

Second, the news of my termination would break Monday morning. I had lived in a secret world all weekend; had celebrated with my friends; but now, I would have to face the heat. My dark, shameful reality was about to reveal itself. Nerves rushed through my veins. I would soon learn what the Charlotte community really thought about me. I knew in my gut that everyone would be happy to see me gone. I envisioned the public relieved, as they'd finally gotten their wish: Jacinda was off the air.

They no longer would have to listen to my crazy laugh, and horrible slang grammar. They would be free of my argumentative ways. I pictured people laughing at me, as they congratulated the station for the decision to let me go. I tried to pick myself up and formulate a plan to hide my embarrassment. What would I say to people? How would I answer all their questions? One thing was for sure. I would stick to plan A, which was sleep through everything.

As that chapter in radio closed, I was forced to resort to advice John, my previous General Manager, had given. The advice was the result of a situation that had transpired on air. I had filled in for a woman who was on maternity leave. I was the complete opposite of her. She was like a sweet Kelly Ripa. I, on the other hand, was more like a Wendy Williams.

I had a spit-fire, saucy, bold, personality. When it comes

to listeners, many of them grow with the on-air radio personalities. They become friends with the people they tune into every morning. Well, the second I started to fill in for her, people let me have it! I'll never forget the morning a lady called in and said she hated me and my voice. She screamed that she wanted me off the air, because she couldn't stand me.

The other hosts thought this was hilarious and great radio comedy. They laughed; and pointed at me, to talk to her. As I opened my mouth to speak, she started to yell and hung up the phone. At the expense of my feelings, I tried to stir up a chuckle and laugh, but I was completely mortified. I lost all composure and strength in my legs. I was utterly embarrassed, and wanted to run to a corner and cry.

I couldn't believe someone had just told me she hated me on live radio, while thousands of people listened. I was angry. I wanted to go to her house and beat her up. I felt so dumb. After the show, the GM sat me down, and simply told me, "Welcome to radio: Rule number one, develop thick skin."

Endure the Pain

I pass on this sweet advice to you, too. Develop thick skin for life. Everyone is not going to like you. Some will make it their mission to see you suffer. Do not run, hide, cry, and complain. Stand tall. Take a deep breath. Endure the pain. One rule of thumb is, stay true to self.

Anyone who has ever been let go from a job knows life falls into a complete storm of emotions and questions. The first question is always, what's next? Followed by a slew of questions like, "How in the world am I going to eat? How will I pay my bills? How can I survive like this?" I whisper an answer to you with a soft smile: "But God."

Three years prior and now 400 miles away, I was in a similar situation - jobless. Thankfully, I had a new perspective. God did it before, so I knew with confidence, He would do it again. The tough circumstances of life only earned stripes to a bigger reward. I still wear them, boldly. Instead of let worry creep in, I trusted in my faith that God had a bigger plan.

Invisible Little Monster

For the record, I was wrong about how I thought the Charlotte community perceived me. When I woke up that Monday morning, to my amazement, I discovered the negativity that swarmed through my mind, leading up to the announcement, was all false. I actually learned I was loved, adored, and sincerely missed. Petitions were even launched, by listeners, to get me back on the air.

While I expected ridicule, embarrassment, and prepared for my hurt and pain, it was actually the opposite that took place. This goes to show the power of a thought.
Many times, we craft up worry and doubt, which then leads to anxiety and depression. Really, it all starts in our little mind. Stop! We have created a monster that doesn't even exist.

Adapt this new rule in life: No worries about anything that hasn't happened. No crying over the possible cancer scare.

No worrying about the exam grade you have not received. No fear about the costly car repair you may not need. Do not tremble when you consider if he/she loves you or not. Do not allow for any negative thoughts to creep into your mind. Until it presents itself as fact, you must stay positive. Remain calm until the doctor calls you with the update. Who knows? The doctor may have good news.

WHAT'S YOUR DASH?

The dash I refer to is the tiny, little line that will be on your tombstone. For this activity, we again, travel to the dark side. The dash will be placed in-between the year you were born and the year you die {i.e. 1975-2037}. The dash represents everything you accomplished. It represents the mark you left behind; and what you are remembered for. It represents who you touched and empowered. The dash speaks volumes, even though it's a tiny, little line. I ask you: What's Your Dash?

If you're not satisfied with what your dash represents today, it's quite alright. Thanks be unto God; you have time to turn your life around. Make your dash powerful and impactful!

List what your dash represents to you, right now. Then, list the steps to accomplish growth in every area. The chapters ahead will sharpen your craft and help you stay on the path to peace and joy. Write down techniques, ideas, dreams, and goals to make your dash more powerful. There's always room for improvement. The vision must be written down before it can become crystal clear. Habakkuk 2:2 says, "The Lord said to me, "Write my answer plainly on tablets, so that a runner can carry the correct message to others."

List what your dash represents:

____

____

List areas of growth & improvement:

____

____

6

FORCED NEW OPPORTUNITY

ISAIAH 41:10

"So do not fear, for I am with you; do not be dismayed, for I am your God. I will strengthen you and help you; I will uphold you with My righteous right hand."

It would thrill me to dance in the dark with the devil. It lit a flame that burned within me. It was a fire I'd carried since I was a little girl. I had no answers as to why I had the desire to do wrong. I knew the things I was doing weren't Christ-like, but the devil had a hold on me. Truthfully, I wasn't sure I was ready for him to let me go.

God is a God of forgiveness. He never held my shortcomings against me. It wasn't until I truly surrendered my all to Him, that I felt the power of His grace. If God can clean someone like me, He can do the same for you.

Mark 11:24

"Therefore, I say to you, all things for which you pray and ask, believe that you have received them and they shall be granted to you."

I Finally Quit

There was one more thing I needed to clean up, if I was going to succeed in life. I was a 14-year-old pot head, turned full-grown woman with an addiction. In my dance with the devil, I finally stepped on his toes. A TV station wanted to hire me! I was beyond excited, but I had hurdles to jump over and these were mountains only God could carry me across.

George, the News Director, called me in for an interview for the new Traffic Reporter position. I blankly stared at him from across his office when he asked for my nonexistent TV reel. I didn't have much TV experience, so I didn't have a reel to show him. I only had a radio air check. My mind raced frantically. This was my only shot!

Then it hit me, maybe I could show him my church announcement videos. He let me pull up my YouTube channel on his computer. Mind you, I had randomly created it just two days prior. On this channel, I had numerous videos that promote church events, service times and sermon series themes. He watched each one as I read scripts from a teleprompter and stood in front of a green screen.

I don't know how it happened, but those videos somehow sealed the deal for him. George wanted to hire me. I was literally about to get this Traffic Reporter job based on my volunteerism at church. Wow! Then, I hit the second roadblock. George uttered these next words. "You will have to take a drug test; I know how you radio people are."

I should share with you that I had cleaned up many things in my life up to this point, but smoking weed was not one of them. I believed this job was destined to be mine, if only I could pass the drug test. That's when God spoke to me in the loudest, yet, softest tone I had ever heard. God said at that very instance, "You can continue to fight the battle with smoking, or you can let it go forever. For I have something large in store for you, more than your mind can comprehend. You will leave a lasting imprint on this world. Right now, you must make a choice."

I put down what I was smoking, at that moment, never to pick it up again. The cravings left, instantly. My old life was dying, by the second, and my new life began to gain strength.

When we ask God to put His hands on the wheel and drive, that means we have to release our hands. To surrender everything to God means everything. This is the hardest part for us, as believers.

In order to see or feel God move, you must let go from those negative things you cling to. Only you know what needs to be removed from your life. There are times when God will shake your foundation and force you to make uncomfortable decisions.

Hair & Make-Up

It was by the grace of God that I passed the drug test, and I received my first on-air television job. This happened only six months after being let go from the radio station. I got the job even though I had no true experience, as a reporter. I began as a Traffic Reporter, and helped to kick off the first 4pm newscast in the Charlotte area. This, as you can imagine, was a huge transition from radio. Not only did I have to sound the part, which meant no more slang or trash talk, I also had to look like I belonged in television. I was required to say goodbye to my long hair and chop it into a short, bob hairstyle.

Special thanks to a good friend, Brigida Mack, a TV veteran, who taught me how to dress and 'beat my face' - that's what she would call flawless makeup. I spent countless hours to tailor my look so I would be camera ready. I had an allotted amount of time to get beautified. This was hard to overcome, as I was somewhat of a tomboy. I now had to do my own hair and makeup, every single day. The big necklaces, earrings, high heels, stylish and classy suits were all part of the job.

As I walked into this new phase, I prayed profusely for God to be my words and mannerisms. There was no way I could do live TV, without Him. I had no idea why God had me there. More importantly, I had no idea what I was doing. Television had never been on my radar; it was just an idea. When it actually happened, I repeatedly asked myself, "What did I get myself into?"

3, 2, 1 Action

I was so nervous when I first appeared on TV, I thought I would pee in my pants, literally. I watched the meteorologist give his forecast. I stood on the other side of the studio and waited for the red light to pop on my camera. The red light indicated I was live. I didn't know how to use my hands, where to look, or what screens to pull up for my traffic report. I could hear producers as they talked in my ear through an earpiece.

All of this went on in my mind, as I tried to relay information to the viewers on air. I was completely freaked out! The only thing I knew, for sure, was that my hands were clammy. I sweated uncontrollably. On top of it all, I balanced myself on a box, as I wore high heels, because I was not tall enough for the camera.

When I saw the light turn red, I thought I would faint right where I stood! All thanks to God, my lips began to move and words began to flow from my mouth. Don't ask me what I said. I don't remember a single thing. My hands shook so badly. It was so terrible that my girlfriend Liz, who trained me, had to type the new updates into all the computers for me. If she hadn't, I would've missed my next traffic hit, due to nervousness.

The Best Advice

God's grace and mercy enabled me to get pretty good at the gig. I received some great advice from people who had been in the business for a long time. They shared their brilliant insight with me. I believe that helped shape my growth in the industry. I carry these nuggets of wisdom with me, and share them with others every chance I get. The best advice, and greatest piece of knowledge I've ever received is, "Don't try to be perfect, because you will always mess up. True talent comes from how well you recover when you do make a mistake."

This advice goes for you, too. Let's face it. We all make mistakes, from time to time. Don't try to be the person who has it all together. We all know this person does not exist. Learn how to rebound when you do fall. True expertise comes in how well you recover. Real character is discovered when a person takes a nosedive to the ground; grabs the railing and stands back up, taller than before the stumble.

"Success consists of going from failure to failure without loss of enthusiasm."

WINSTON CHURCHILL

I became extremely comfortable in my craft, able to relax and have fun. My goal was to develop a personal relationship with each person who sat on the other side of the TV. I wanted to provide transparency and quality information, sprinkled with my spunky personality. There's something special when you connect with a person through television.

The best part about this new opportunity was, I noticed it was my radio experience that helped prepare me for the television industry. The countless hours of reading copy, improv classes, and daily air check sessions after each radio show, equipped me to be natural, funny, and relatable on TV. The truth is, it all paid off, in that new season. Every season of your life prepares you for the next one.

Everything you go through builds you up for the next journey. It doesn't matter how much you may hate where you are at this very second. Don't get caught up on how uncomfortable it is, you will one day be grateful for it all. It is all a part of the process, to shape your life and your walk. Where you are, right now, is a bridge set to connect you to your next phase. The difficult part is you will not know what you learned until you've transitioned. Hindsight is 20/20, you can always see the lessons clear, after they become the past.

Another Broken Road

The "high" of reporting traffic soon began to wear off. I was ready to grow into bigger ventures, and take my talent into new territory.

My friend Sarah told me about a television station nearby that was hiring. She demanded I call ASAP. I mean, literally. She left the studio for a few minutes, and came back to ask if I had inquired, yet. Sarah was on me pretty hard, so I felt the nudge to apply, immediately. I went into the parking lot and sat in my car to call the News Director. By lunchtime, I had a scheduled meeting with him. Things happened so fast, I didn't really have time to think.

That was my life. I searched for peace, happiness, and purpose on dead end streets. My bosses would say how happy they were with my work. Viewers would write in with such kind words. From the outside, it looked like I had won. It smelled like sparkling success. For reasons I could not understand, I was still dying inside. I was climbing up the media ladder, with no end in sight and without any genuine passion. I was trying to fill a void with a job that no career, amount of money, or corporate gain could give.

Sometimes, it's not the job that's the problem. It's you. You jump from job to job and constantly look for the next best thing. However, if you don't fix yourself first, you will always be left empty inside.

PRAYER LIFE

Jeremiah 29:12

"Then you will call on Me and come and pray to Me, and I will listen to you."

When you wake up, pray. Before you eat, pray a prayer of thankfulness. Take a step further- pray before everything! Pray before you give a speech. Pray for God to give you the words, thoughts, and mannerisms. Pray for people to see His face, not yours. Pray for God to do supernatural wonders through you.

Pray before you have to take a test. Pray for God to give you every answer. Leave it all up to God. Pray to God to have His way in your life. Take yourself out of the equation, and let God show His hand. His abilities are limitless. Take your hand off the wheel and let God steer for you.

When you learn to pray first, it ensures God will walk with you every second of the day. Pray before everything. Do not try to do anything on your own. Let your days be filled with continuous, ongoing prayer with your Lord and Savior.

One easy way for you to make sure you never miss another prayer time - set a prayer alarm. These prayer alarms can be themed. For instance, the 7:00am alarm will be for guidance through the day. The 12pm prayer will be for gratefulness, and a prayer of blessings over everyone who walks in your path. Or you can simply set alarms that will remind you to say a prayer to God for any concern on your heart.

To take it a step further, you can also set prayer alarms with family and friends. When the alarm goes off, take that time to pray together. It may be a quiet prayer, whispered under your breath. Or, you may find yourself alone, and able to dive deeply into a more in-depth time with God.

Either way, prayer time with a friend helps you realize you are not alone. This prayer warrior can be in another part of the world, but when that alarm goes off, they will be right there with you. They will stand in the gap with you and pray on your behalf.

I also highly recommend couples have set prayer alarms. This is a special time in the day that only you two will share. It's not for the kids, your finances, your home or career. This is a time that you pray favor over his/her life.

A Strengthened Prayer

Prayer is extremely important for your spiritual growth. You can pray quietly throughout the day, or you can shout with praise. It's important to remember prayer is simply constant communication with God. It can and will truly change your circumstances. Stand firmly on prayer throughout your faith journey.

One tip I'd like to recommend is to write down your

prayers. I developed this routine as a child. When I was in elementary school, I had a diary with a little lock on it. I would write down who I had a crush on, and what my grades were, at the time. I also wrote about slumber parties and friendships. My diary had all the juice. As I got older, and started to really experience life, my diary turned into a journal, which then turned to a book of prayers to God.

Prayer Journal

A prayer journal is also a great tool to express yourself and stay in constant communication with God. Write down your thoughts, fears, worries, and doubts. Express gratefulness. Pray for those around you. Pray for those who you may not even know. Pray for yourself, and for your family. Just let your hand go and begin to write. When you write down your prayers, you can then look back and see how far you've come. It will bring a smile to your face to see how far God has brought you.

Your Prayer Journal Starts Now!

Date:

Dear Lord,

7

A VICIOUS CYCLE

1 CORINTHIANS 9:24

"Do you not know that in a race all the runners run, but only one receives the prize? So run that you may obtain it."

Within a couple of weeks, I had become a weather forecaster and reporter, for a totally different television station. This was another opportunity where God promoted me, without having any true television experience. Where was God taking me?

Look back over your life. I'm sure there were circumstances where you felt you were not qualified. Sometimes, you do not look qualified on paper. Whether it be your age, or lack of experience, God has already qualified you. When He opens the door, walk in.

In most professions, you need a resume to prove your background. Some may even require certifications and accolades. In television, news directors request a television reel. A reel, is a collection of work that showcases the applicant's talents and abilities. Remember, I got my first television job from church announcements videos. As I write this book, I have worked in television for many years; and hosted numerous events. Yet, I didn't create a television reel until 2016. God already qualified me.

Allow God to do the impossible in your life. Stand firm on your faith, God has qualified you, as well. You are Uniquely Qualified, my love.

Forecasting Clouds

What the heck is a cumulous cloud, anyway? I am the type of person to walk outside, wave my hand back and forth; and take a wild guess what the temperature is. Now, in my new position, I was responsible for accurate delivery of weather forecasts, without an ounce of experience. This, by the way, is one of the most important positions to hold in television. Talk about pressure!

On my first day, I knew it was not going to be an easy transition, like previous jobs. My mind felt like it would explode. It was like a loud, tornado siren alerting of imminent danger. It was as though I predicted severe weather in my own life. I knew, this time, I could not continue to run. Even though something did not sit well with me, I gulped and signed a three-year contract. Regardless of whether I enjoyed reporting weather or not, there was no way out, this time.

Reporting the weather was exciting. Who knew? I stood in front of a camera for three minutes to talk about the skies. It took me back down memory lane, to when I would give presentations in high school. I thoroughly enjoyed every second of it! In a nutshell, anchors tossed to me, then I would share the one thing to make or break a viewer's day. Weather impacts us all, in some form or fashion. I enjoyed the time with viewers.

For once, it felt like I delivered useful information, rather than solely talk about the latest gossip. I provided a service. People wanted to know if they could wash their car or cut the grass. They wanted to know if conditions were safe to drive their kids to school. People turned on their television to plan their life, and I was a huge part of it. How ironic I was hired to forecast clouds, rain and storms, when my life was a torrential down pour of watches and warnings.

But Reporting...

Reporting news, on the other hand, was extremely difficult. I consider myself a writer, but more so, a writer of the heart. The journalistic style of local news is a different story. In addition, I had absolutely no idea that the role of a reporter was a 24/7 job. I would roll out of bed, to find my inbox full of emails for potential story leads. My stomach would be in knots all morning, if I didn't have a confirmed story locked in.

Our editorial meetings were the worst part of it all for me. They were a complete nightmare. Editorial meetings were like "Sales 101." I had to sell my bosses on why certain stories were important to the community. From there, the producers and news director would stack the newscasts with potential stories they wanted to air.

I never delivered my story pitch correctly. I would always

start off with, "I know you're not going to like this idea, but this is what I have." My co-workers would laugh at me. They said I needed to have more confidence in my pitch. I would speak defeat before I even presented my pitch.

Every day, they would assign me a story to report on. I would be sent out into the field to capture the interviews. This meant, I would jump in the station vehicle and run around the city and interview different people. I would have to grab b-roll footage, which are video clips used to help tell the story. Every day was completely different. I had no idea where I would end up. I was constantly thrown into different, excruciating elements, such as blistering heat, downpours, and freezing temperatures. The environment didn't matter. The story just needed to be told.

Whether people would talk on camera was another factor that impacted my report. Many people would speak with me and share their point of view. However, very few would share on camera. This was a big obstacle I had to overcome. Every day I internally screamed, "I have a college degree for crying out loud! Why am begging strangers to talk on camera." I had no idea half of this job was consisted of sales techniques. It took a special, acquired skill to get someone to share information on camera, for thousands to see. The only rule: I couldn't return to the newsroom empty handed.

This position also required that my attire be business casual, yet prepared for anything. Food was certainly on the go. Many times, I didn't have time to eat. It was a race against the clock. I had to interview, write, and edit the story, on a tight deadline. My goodness, the pressure was through the roof! Once the story aired, my stomach would be in knots. Did people like the story? Was it received well? Were there any errors? But, I could no longer dwell on that story. It was time to think about that new story - The story I needed to pitch tomorrow, in the editorial meeting.

I worked strenuous hours, weekends, and holidays. Never forget this, when you're at home with your family on Christmas Day, the news still goes on. There were many weeks I worked without any days off. The job wasn't as glamorous as I thought.

After a while, the work became extremely difficult. Unlike other reporters and anchors, I did not have that twinkle in my eyes for news. The people who do it, have dreamed of doing it their entire lives. For me, God just put me there for reasons I did not know.

Here's the kicker. Everywhere I went, people would say, "Oh, my goodness! You're on TV; you must be so happy!" To the outside world, I had made it. But, on the inside, I yelled at the top of my lungs, "I HATE THIS!" I was in deep trouble this time, and I saw no way out. In response, I just smiled with my infamous, rehearsed line, "This is a great opportunity and I'm learning a lot." Hey, that was my truth.

Losing Myself

My personal life started to crumble once I committed to a life of reporting. Before I knew it, everything slowly revolved around the next story. After a couple years, my friends no longer invited me places. They knew I was always tied up with work. The idea of a balanced work, family, and friends' lifestyle was nonexistent. I was supposed to enjoy life. I was in my 20s. But, I felt trapped in a contract, with nowhere to turn. I began to hate work and felt lonely at home. It was like every part of my life suffered. Over time, I suffocated. I completely lost myself.

Google Search

I was in media for so long, that I had no experience or contacts in any other field of work. I felt stuck to my degree, work experiences, and years of dedication. Finally, I hit a brick wall. I couldn't bear to stand another minute. I felt as if I had no other option. It was a low, dark place to be.

You know what messed me up the most? I thought about the people who really wanted my job. This was someone else's dream job and I was in the way. I felt horrible. It made me imagine, what if everyone worked in their passion? How wonderful life would be!

I searched online for other potential jobs. Each time, I would find myself in front of a blank screen, unsure of what to type in the search box.

If you do not know where to turn, this is a sure sign it's not time for you to leave, just yet. Unfortunately for you, there is more work to be done. There's a person you are supposed to encounter; an experience you're supposed to have.

Just Breathe

Have you ever felt like you couldn't breathe? As if life sucked all the air out of your lungs? These are the hardest times to endure. But, they become the experiences that change you the most. Think about the most horrific experiences you've ever had. Now think of the blessings that spawned from these experiences. If you are currently in the storm of your life, I encourage you to step out of your own circumstances for one second.

See that God is in control. Believe that He will bring you through it. You are being groomed for greatness. You are being taken through the trenches and developed for success. Even when you can't breathe, whisper, "Thank You, God."

It was at this fork in the road that I began to ask myself, "Have I come too far to walk away?" Yes, I had come pretty far, but not to give up. It was time to apply what I learned from all the many experiences and previous jobs. Nothing was wasted.

"Mistakes become lessons. Pain becomes purpose. A mess becomes a message. A test becomes a testimony. Every struggle has opportunity. No matter how bad your situation is, get a lesson from it."

Tony A. Gaskins

SQUARE PEG, ROUND HOLE

Can you fit a square peg in a round hole? No. It simply will not fit. This reminds me of an activity toddlers use when they try to learn new shapes. Parents will give them a board filled with holes cut into different shapes and sizes. Then, they will give their children separate blocks that fit perfectly into each slot. Kids will typically struggle, as they place the objects in all the wrong places. They may have a circular shape, but try to force it into the square slot. What they will learn is the circle shape does not fit in the square slot, and, it never will.

This is a simple learning technique, but it applies to us, even today. We are constantly in search of where we fit in. For some of us, it takes a long time to learn. Everything in life operates in God's timing. He will make the pieces fit perfectly. Stop fighting circumstances that, simply, do not fit. They don't fit for a reason. Trust in His magnificent timing. You will one day fit perfectly, and be placed exactly where you're supposed to be.

8

TRUE AUTHENTIC SELF

ROMANS 12:2

"Do not be conformed to this world, but be transformed by the renewal of your mind, that by testing you may discern what is the will of God, what is good and acceptable and perfect."

I once covered a story of how local weather conditions impacted the livelihood of strawberry farmers. Yes, this was the highlight of my weather-related stories. As I covered the story for news, I started to ask some personal questions to the farmer and his wife. They shared with me that growing strawberries was a gamble. If temperatures got too cold, their entire crop could be ruined, and thousands of dollars would be lost. The more time I spent with them, I learned they were former engineers who had inherited the farm land.

Here were two people who had built careers as engineers, and decided to give it all up for strawberries. The sweetest part for them was they had no guarantee for success. It was just two people who decided to follow their passion. They wanted to go back to the root of their love, to live on a farm. They ran lights, thermometers, and sprinkler systems throughout their farmland.

If temperatures grew too cold, the thermometer would signal the sprinkler system to water the strawberries. This kept them from freezing. An intricate system set up inside of their home would alert them if they needed to tend to their berries. They decided to take their engineering expertise and incorporate it into the strawberry business.

God used their testimony to plant a seed in my heart. Here they were 20-30 years deep into a career, and decided to leave it, to try something new. Their story sparked hope within me. I wondered if I could do the same.

Would you be able to walk away, too? Could you take everything acquired up to this point, and use it to enhance and prepare your next season? Follow your passion; it will lead you to your purpose.

Authenticity Revealed

In order to find out what lies ahead of you, you must first do a serious analysis of yourself. Tap into the deepest part of your soul. It's time to come face-to-face with your authentic self. You may have spent years in development of the life you think you want. But, once all is said and done, you may find out you don't like any of it. You may have a great family, nice car, house, and career. However, you may still feel empty inside.

Let Me Be Me

Here's a story of another couple who inspired me to look in the mirror, at myself. Nate and Leslie said the first few years of their marriage were difficult. Leslie had become extremely successful in her company. She moved all the way up the ranks, until she worked herself to the top. Then, Leslie began to come home with new job opportunities for her husband. It was her hope that Nate, too, would walk into a top position, as she had. Leslie rubbed elbows with powerful people, daily.

One simple phone call could secure a successful career for Nate. This would be beneficial for both him, and their family, she thought. Time and time again, this would spark a disagreement between them. She didn't understand why, but Nate's perspective was much different from hers. He was a lover of the simple things in life. He loved to teach. His salary was significantly less than hers; but he loved his profession and couldn't see himself doing anything else.

To sit with the bigwigs, or to have a new job opportunity, never interested him. To her, it may have looked as though Nate had just a job, not necessarily a career. It may have appeared that he was only in his current job until something better popped up. To Leslie, it looked like her husband needed a better job, one that would produce more income, with upward mobility.

However, Nate had come face-to-face with his true, authentic self. He eventually told her, "I am very happy right where I am. I know this doesn't pay much, but I am okay. I need you to be okay, too." It was at that moment he became comfortable in his own skin. He was happy when he wore his relaxed, loose-fitted clothes.

Some of his clothes were seasoned and torn, but Nate preferred those versus fancy, tailored suits. He found peace as he made a difference in the lives of children. This was a powerful turning point in their relationship. They had finally understood and respected each other's journey, never to push in separate directions again.

CONSIDER YOUR PEACE

Consider your peace. What does your true, authentic self look like? Write it down and be as descriptive as possible. What are your likes, wants, needs, and deepest desires? Do not incorporate what others will think or say about you; this especially includes the opinions of family and friends. With every decision, ask yourself one important question: "Will this bring me joy?"

What does my authentic self look like? Describe.

____

____

____

____

____

____

____

____

____

____

____

____

____

____

____

____

____

9

THE STIRRING

EPHESIANS 6:12

"For our struggle is not against flesh and blood,
but against the rulers, against the authorities,
against the powers of this dark world and against
the spiritual forces of evil in the heavenly realms."

The worst experience of my life was when I was forced to endure the "stirring." The best way to describe it: I was unable to breathe. I was completely trapped. The stirring was dark and uncomfortable. Even when I fought back, it took over every part of my body. No matter how hard I tried, it felt as though steel slowly consumed me. As I sat at my desk, these thoughts would hit me like bullets. I needed to comprehend how I felt, but was overwhelmed. I wanted it all to end. This chapter will describe the emotions I experienced throughout this dark period.

"It seeped into my blood like black ooze, lava,
or even coal ash. It slowly took over my body

and mind, and left me breathless. I tried to
take a deep breath, but it felt as if I couldn't
breathe. I lost the ground from under my feet.
I could not think straight. All hope was lost."

JACINDA JACOBS

CHINO

As a little girl, I had a family dog named Chino. He was a dark brown and black lab mix, I think. He was the cutest little puppy ever. Since my parents loved cappuccino, we decided to name our dog Chino. One afternoon, as I walked Chino down my neighborhood street of Keeton Court, something caught his eye. He took off, full speed ahead. I felt my nerves rush to my throat, because I knew there was no way I could keep up with his speed. Immediate thoughts rushed through my mind.

"Do I let go of the leash, or do I let him drag me down the street?" Either way, I had already lost this battle. My thoughts were not fast enough. I heard the leash run out. In a flash, Chino was gone, and the leash snapped off of his collar. It jammed back in my direction. I gulped for air, as the leash made full impact.

With all its force, the leash hit directly in the middle of my chest. The impact took my breath away. I tried to gasp for air, but I couldn't. Everything stopped, in slow motion. I had the wind knocked out of me.

Imagine this constant banter of breathlessness creep into your world, daily. This is what "the stirring" feels like. I'm sure I don't have to explain this to you, in much more detail. You know very well what suffocation feels like. It's one of the reason you continue to turn the pages to this book.

Chicken Noodle Soup

The stirring season does not feel good, but it's needed. This process will shape and mold you for greatness. The stirring will strengthen you.

Did your mom ever make homemade soup for you as a child? My mom didn't, so I can't use this example from my own personal experience. When I think of how the stirring process shapes us, I think of a bowl of chicken noodle soup. Think of all the ingredients - chicken, noodles, celery, carrots, chicken broth, water, and anything else special your mom may have used to make it.

Again, we used Campbell's, so flatter me a bit. I'm really reaching here! These ingredients are essential to a magnificent bowl of chicken noodle soup. However, all of these ingredients separately will not make soup. In addition, if these ingredients are left cold, you would not be able to enjoy a bowl of hot soup. It's only when all of these ingredients come together, boil, and simmer in the fire, that soup is made.

The fire represents the stirring process. These ingredients must undergo the fire. It's not possible to make a bowl of hot soup without the heat. The stirring process can't be skipped and it can't be rushed. It's a crucial step, but once completed, you will enjoy a flavorful and hearty bowl of chicken noodle soup.

A powerful observation about this darkness is it allows you to grow closer to God. This, my friend, is the main reason for your storm - God wants you to lean on Him. Sometimes, God will bring you out of the storm, other times, He will let the storm rage, but give you peace through it.

This transition means old debris is burnt off and removed so new growth and purpose can shine. This stirring period develops you. You are forced to lean on God for your every breath. It's the most uncomfortable period, but it's the most valuable. Allow your spirit to undergo this journey. Don't fight it. Accept the transformation.

On Second Thought, Let's Blow This Joint

I vividly remember the constant array of thoughts, to grab my purse and run. I thought to myself, "What's the worst that could happen?" I wasn't breaking the law, so no one could throw me in jail, if I walked off the job. Yes, my name would be smeared throughout the media industry, but that didn't matter. I needed out. I wanted to run for the hills, and flee as far away as possible. I would have rather started over, then finish what I started.

I started to throw around the idea of a part-time job. I considered work as a waitress, while I figured out my next move. I needed to swallow my humility. I sat in my living room one night and began to look around my home. I loved my house. I had just purchased a car, also. Was I ready to give this all up? I would need to downgrade my lifestyle. This would be the result of a situation I caused myself. Were a few bad days worth risking it all?

Forced Choices

God used a close friend of mine to speak life into me. My friend had lost everything he'd ever worked for, as his business abruptly closed. He thought he had enough money saved up in case of an emergency, but it was wiped out in less than two months. Life's curveball threw him out of the game. Constant worry became an instinct for him, just as his next breath. This scared me to my soul, as I, ultimately, volunteered to walk into a similar lifestyle as his.

Dreaded Advice

I knew I needed to reach out for some guidance and decided to contact Jennifer, an acquaintance of mine. I barely knew her on a personal level, but for years had heard nothing but good things about her. From her service to others, I could see she was on fire for God. She was a previous News Anchor at my first TV station. I'll never forget when I first got my email account set up, her farewell email to the staff was one of the first emails to hit my inbox.

The email was detailed and heartfelt. She shared with everyone that she had finally answered the call and was excited to switch careers from media to ministry. My spirit led me to her. I felt if anyone could understand my cry it would be her.

One rainy afternoon, I sat in my car on the phone, as she listened to my story. Jennifer's first piece of advice was to honor God. She reminded me to take heed to God's plan. She told me there was a reason I was at that job. She told me the words I had dreaded, "You cannot run this time."

She explained to me that I could not leave until I had completed His assignment. This was not what I wanted to hear. I wanted to run. I needed someone to tell me to run like the wind! Yet, she said the opposite. I lied, when I told her I understood, as I hung up.

Keep in mind, your journey is a process. It will not end when you want it to. Sadly, you may have a couple months to go, or even a few years, before you reach the personal freedom you dream of. During this time, be on the lookout for wise souls who will speak life into your situation. These people will go against the grain. They will tell you what you need to hear, not just what you want to hear.

No matter how much I didn't like it, she was right. It was because of her own walk, experience, and wisdom, that she could imprint value and substance upon my heart. I needed to wait on God.

"Many of life's failures are people who
did not realize how close they were
to success when they gave up."

THOMAS EDISON

GIVE IT A NAME

Life will throw you tests, daily. If you notice some of the tests are reoccurring, it's because you have not successfully passed them. Some of us will fail the same tests, for years. Remember this, if you fail the test, be ready to repeat it. These tests may come in different variations like jobs, relationships, or finances. At times, you fail, because you can't identify the lesson when it happens.

Here's one way to identify a test - Give it a name. It's important for you to be aware of the lesson every time it presents itself. For example, you may find yourself in a frenzy when someone cuts you off on the highway. The best way to prepare yourself for this lesson is to give it a name. Name it something like, I don't know, "Larry," for instance. The next time you get cut off, calmly remind yourself that this is the "Larry" test. Identify it. Recognize it. Then, calmly let the driver have the lane, while you remain in peace.

You may fight with tests of a sharp tongue, and go off at a split second. Name this test, "The Flip Out Test." Maybe your test is that you talk too much. Let's label this test, "The Gabby Test." Maybe you try too hard to control everything. This test can be called, "The Control Freak Test." Take heed to your tests. What tests have you had to repeat? Give them a name so you can pass, not fail, the next time they show up.

10

FLOWER BLOOM

EPHESIANS 1:18

"I pray that the eyes of your heart may be enlightened in order that you may know the hope to which He has called you, the riches of His glorious inheritance in His Holy people."

After a short-lived wait on God, I went right back to wanting to quit. For some reason, I found solace as I complained and gloated in my deep, dark world. I had been at this point for way too long. I no longer had the courage or strength to see any good in that television job. I didn't know how to smile anymore, until God revealed the beauty I couldn't see.

OPERATION: KEEP FLOWERS ALIVE

When I moved into my new home, the first thing I wanted to do was plant beautiful flowers in the front yard. I had always dreamed of playing music, sipping iced tea, and having a fun-filled day in the garden. When I attempted to do this myself, the experience completely sucked. I broke my shovel. It was hot and muggy. I had inchworms in my hair and clothes. The bags of mulch were extremely heavy, and hurt my back. The ground was rock solid. I had to fight with every dig to get those stinking flowers in.

I began to get frustrated and irritated. This was nothing like I had envisioned. I couldn't wait to be finished with that dumb task. Finally, hours later and a day wasted, I finished. I did it. I took a few steps back, and gleamed with joy and amazement. I now had beautiful flowers in front of my new home. My happiness was short lived, however.

I noticed all of the flowers started to die, in the weeks that followed. In my ignorance, I had no idea that some flowers loved the sunshine, while others didn't. Certain flowers needed extra water; and others didn't need much water at all. Oh, my goodness!

Every day, I set an early alarm to get up and start the sprinkler. I would pull into the driveway with my eyes glued on the status of my flowers. I almost ran into the garage door one time, I was so focused. It became my summer battle. I called it, "Operation: Keep Flowers Alive."

Over time, I lost the battle. Every week, another stem would shrivel up and die. My front yard went from a beautiful landscape to a horrible eyesore. I didn't know what else to do. I gave up. I felt defeated. I was angry. I wanted to pull them all up, but I couldn't. I was connected to those flowers. That is, until one rainy, cool, August morning.

A photographer came to the house to take my roommate's engagement pictures. Later that day, she sent me a lone picture of one of the flowers. When I opened the attachment, I saw one of the most beautiful sights I had ever seen. The picture showed a tiny daisy with yellow petals. The strong stem gleamed with bright green leaves. Each petal glistened with little droplets of rain.

I was speechless. How in the world had this come from that flowerbed? God said, "This beauty had been there all along. You just chose not to see it." My God! I only chose to fix my eyes on the broken leaves and withered flowers. I only saw death and never took the time to notice there was still life in that flowerbed. I had grown entirely too comfortable with complaining. I couldn't see the blessings God had placed there, all along.

I encourage you to open your eyes. See what God has for you. I promise you it's there. You may not have been able to notice it yet, but there's beauty in your midst. Be wise. Fix your eyes on God's blessing.

Impossible Possible

One Sunday, I was in church, and the Lord impressed something deep in my soul. As I cried and praised Him, I felt God say, "It's time to share how you feel with your boss." Can you believe it? My dream had come true. I would finally be able to leave. Mentally, my bags were already packed. My desk stayed empty. I knew I wouldn't occupy that space for very long, so I never decorated it, to begin with. I was excited. God had revealed the answer to my prayers. This is what I had waited for. Little did I know, I had misinterpreted the message.

I waited years for God to reveal these words to me, so

of course, I eagerly obeyed. I marched right into work and asked Kevin, my boss, if I could have a word with him. After I closed his office door, Kevin sat straight up from behind his desk. He was confused and wanted to hear what I needed to get off my chest. I had his undivided attention.

Then, I did it. I informed him that I was not happy. I shared my dissatisfaction with my current position. I poured my empty heart to Kevin. To share concerns of this magnitude was a definite risk. I was well aware of this, but the time was now. I immediately became a liability for the station. I was scared, yet, I was bold.

Initially, Kevin was not happy with my dissatisfaction. He shared with me that he had no idea I was unhappy. He told me that he and management were all pleased with my work. He asked me, "What can I do to make this work?" I simply explained to him that I needed to do stories that had purpose. I wanted my career to be connected to my calling. My heart yearned to be more involved in the community.

Kevin sat in silence. I waited. Then, he told me, "What if I give you the opportunity to turn one, positive community story, a week?" My heart skipped a beat. This meant I would be able to spotlight a nonprofit and provide a voice to those community angels we rarely get to see. I was given the privilege to inspire others and share their stories of hope.

I was scared. I was fearful. I expected to get fired. But, look at God. God is a great God. When you are open and honest, and share your heart, others will receive it. This glorious moment felt like God had slowly shifted my life. He changed the unchangeable. God showed me that He would eventually use my media talents for His glory.

Psalm 37:4

"Delight yourself in the Lord; And He will give you the desires of your heart."

Confirmation

As I turned to leave Kevin's office, and walk toward my cubicle, my desk phone rang. It was pretty rare to hear the phone ring. I was usually out in the field. I decided to pick it up, anyways. Both good and bad news were on the line. The bad news was my camera crew had been denied approval for a story I'd been assigned to, that day. That was a bummer, because I was then, out of a story, and Sundays were slow news days.

Before I hung up the phone, I received the good news. The lady said, "Jacinda, if you're ever looking for a positive story, I have a non profit where we teach kids to step. These choreographed routines include marching and sharp, military style movements. We help build their confidence and keep them off the street. It would make their day if you came out to film them." This became my first community interest story!

I no longer tried to fit the rectangle block into the circle slot. For the first time in my life, everything had begun to fall into its perfect place. I honored God's word. I prayed. I waited. Change had begun to happen.

Glimpse of Hope

Things were not totally fixed at this point, but God had

given a tiny glimpse of hope. This helped me hold on.

Each inspirational story written brought life back to me as a reporter. These stories taught me how to correctly interview, write scripts, and how to effectively tell a story. My greatest gain was that this opportunity allowed me to give back to the community.

One day, I received some great feedback from one of my previously featured, inspirational stories. Mara, The founder of a well-known nonprofit, The Sandbox called to schedule a follow-up story, and shared the good news. Each year, this non-profit relied on limos to escort their patients to a huge, lavish prom.

She explained that the limo company she had hired, pulled out just days before her event the year prior. This left her without transportation. She was forced to scramble for a back-up plan. In the last seconds, she'd hoped to find a new limo company that would help her. Her plan B led her to the perfect company.

As God would have it, the person who answered the phone was familiar with her work in the community. This woman had seen the nonprofit featured in one of my stories. The lady jumped to the occasion, and immediately said her limo company would help. More importantly, she said that they would be honored to serve The Sandbox.

There are no words to tell you how it felt to know that I had a small hand in helping this nonprofit gain recognition for its great works. That was a small butterfly flap in the wind; a tiny shift that ultimately revealed purpose.

MATTHEW 7:7

"Ask, and it will be given to you;
seek, and you will find;
knock, and it will be opened unto you."

HOPEFUL MOMENTS

Moments like these give you optimism of what's yet to come. What are your hopeful moments? Write them down. When you see one pop up, latch onto it. You will start to understand that life is not all bad. This will give you the fuel to keep going.

11

WALK IN LOVE

EPHESIANS 5:2

"And walk in the way of love, just as Christ loved us and gave Himself up for us as a fragrant offering and sacrifice to God."

My father raised me up to be extremely strong and tough. It was more of a requirement than anything else. He demanded that I protect myself, no matter what the cost. For a long time, I thought the quick-tempered person I displayed was the real me. I think it was all a lie, to protect the soft, sweet, kind girl that's inside. In all honesty, was really an emotional person, who loved and cared, deeply.

My father's story is quite different from most. He was born and raised in a large family, in the Dominican Republic.

He had 11 brothers and sisters. The family moved to the United States when he was very young and unable to speak English. Imagine a life where everywhere you go, and everything you do, presents a language barrier. This is what my dad faced when he moved to New York City. He shared stories of how people laughed at him when he spoke incorrectly. It was probably moments like this where he started to develop a rough exterior for himself.

By the time my dad became a parent, one thing was for certain: He was not a sucka. He didn't raise me nor my brothers to be suckas, either. If I'd told my dad I got hit at school, he would have hit me. He was just one of those parents. Judge him all you want, but that was my dad. I respected his stance. He even enrolled me in karate.

My dad wanted us to know how to protect ourselves. He didn't want us to be taken advantage of. My dad raised me to demand respect. He taught me not to let people get by with little things. He believed that if I did, they would try to get by with everything, after that.

I learned this lesson, first hand, when I was in the first or second grade. We lived in Germany, at the time. A neighborhood kid and I were up the hill playing in the dirt. For reasons I can't remember, we got in a fight. The kid had messed with me so much, that I took my bucket and popped him upside his head. He cried and ran home.

Later that night, his parents were at our doorstep, ready to confront my dad. They expected him to be apologetic, but they didn't know my dad. When he learned the complete story, he immediately took my defense. He knew I would not hit anyone for no apparent reason. He told them, "If your kid continues to mess with my daughter, she will continue to knock him upside his head, have a good night." He then closed the door on them. I liked when my dad protected me. My dad's lessons taught me to protect myself, at any cost. If I'd let someone slide an inch, they would eventually come back and take a mile.

Exodus 14:14

"The Lord Himself will fight
for you. Just stay calm."

I understood this philosophy, growing up. However, my viewpoint changed over the years. My walk with Jesus has showed me to be Christ-like. There are times we will fall weak to our flesh, but we are to walk in love. We are to be slow to speak and quick to listen. I learned as an adult, to reflect Jesus' way, instead. God's word teaches us love is the winner, over all things.

There are still times I feel tested, when someone tries to pull a fast one on me. I can hear my father in my head, telling me not to be a sucka. I can feel a rage begin to brew from within, when I feel taken advantage of. For example, I may feel it on the highway from time to time. I may see it in the grocery store if someone tries to cut the line.

You name it, I am ready to go. That's a weakness that I still hold onto, deep down inside; because I don't want others to think I'm a sucka. When in fact, it shouldn't matter what anyone else thinks. The only thing anyone should notice is the God in me.

Nasty Email

An angry viewer emailed me a nasty note. It described my horrible delivery of the weather and detailed a long list of inaccuracies. Well, I put Arthur in his place, as I tactfully addressed every complaint. I went home feeling like a winner. The next morning, however, the Holy Spirit let me know that nothing in that email was Christ-like. This forced me to correct my mistake. I sent a follow-up email to Arthur and apologized for my rude response. As hard as it was to admit, I explained to him that his email hurt my feelings, and that my response was simply to cover up the hurt.

The next day, I received the longest email from Arthur. He expressed to me that his wife had always said his tone and delivery came off as mean. He said he had no intention of hurting my feelings and apologized. Then, Arthur went on to say how much he loved my weather reports. I sat at my desk in amazement. I had no idea we would become friends. That had been just a simple mix up. You would have thought I'd learned my lesson, right?

Flipped Out

My neighbor Mrs. Shirley screamed at me one morning, because my dog walked into her backyard and relieved himself. No! I had no idea my dog Lil Reese's walked his butt all the way over there. I was embarrassed. I felt horrible. I was completely, over-the-top apologetic. I was dead wrong for what transpired. I wanted Mrs. Shirley to know it would never happen again and that I would clean up everything. I apologized profusely, over and over again, but this lady wasn't having it. She still responded harshly.

Then, I felt it begin to bubble up inside of me. I began to feel attacked, which quickly evolved into disrespect. In a snap of a finger, I flipped out on Mrs. Shirley. Just like that, it was over. I screamed back at her. I said every curse word in the book. Since I hadn't cursed in years, it felt kind of good too. I said words that didn't even make sense, just as an excuse to say them. I told her to get off my property. I told her I wouldn't clean anything. I even told her I would purposely walk my dog to her yard tomorrow so he could go to the bathroom. Yeah, I went in on her.

I went inside the house like, "Yeah, I told her." But, the anger festered all day long. I stayed angry for nearly a week. I relived this rage every time I thought of Mrs. Shirley or looked at her house. I couldn't shake it, this anger had a hold on me.

A couple days later, I was with a group of students, and I shared this story with them. Of course, I left out the really bad parts, but I wanted to explain to them that, even as adults, we still make mistakes. The teacher, Mrs. Matthews pulled me aside immediately after class; looked me straight in my eyes and asked me if I had apologized, yet. I continued to justify my actions and snapped back with a stern reply, "No."

Mrs. Matthews explained to me how the battle was never between my neighbor Mrs. Shirley and me. It's actually spiritual warfare that surrounds us daily. She warned me that until I rectified the situation, the devil would continue to have this stronghold over me. I had to let go of my pride. I had to apologize to Mrs. Shirley. I was wrong, no matter what the circumstances.

The next morning, I woke up with an extremely heavy

heart. That was not the person I wanted to be. I wanted to lead by example and to be Christ-like. I wrote a forgiveness letter to Mrs. Shirley and took full responsibility for everything. I apologized for the language, for all the mean hurtful things I said, and more importantly, I apologized for what Lil Reese's had done. It felt like a weight had lifted off of me, the second I stepped up to the plate to admit fault. It was a great lesson. No longer under my father's teaching, I now walked in love.

I placed the forgiveness letter in Mrs. Shirley's mailbox that morning and smiled as I drove off to work. It didn't matter to me if she read the letter or not. I had done my part and it felt good. A week later, I received a forgiveness letter from Mrs. Shirley. "All was forgiven" it read, signed, "President of HOA." What?! I had no idea she led the Homeowners Association. Thank the Lord I was able to smooth things over her. She could have made my life a complete nightmare.

We often get nasty with others out of fear. It's the best way to cover up insecurity, vulnerability, and weakness. Learn to admit when someone has hurt you; otherwise, it can and will cause unnecessary pain. Show love in all your actions. When you experience negativity, activate your Holy Spirit. Allow Him to stir up mighty power inside of you.

And when you mess up, apologize immediately for your indiscretions. Be creative. Send heartfelt letters, gifts, or ask for forgiveness face-to-face. You will quickly regain control of the situation, within seconds. Humble yourself and take immediate notice of your wrongdoing. Do not allow a spirit of arrogance to encumber you. Immediately free yourself from the bondage of Satan's suffocating ways. You may feel embarrassed, and appear to be the loser in the fight, but, in fact, you are the victor!

FORK IN THE ROAD

When was the last time you were tested? I mean, truly challenged. One of those experiences when you say to yourself, "I'm saved, but I will go there with you, if you try me."

Did you pass or did you fail that test? Did you show God's grace? Did you display God's ever forgiving mercy in your words, and in your actions? Do you feel good with the choices you made?

If you failed this test, ask yourself what could you have done differently. It's important to address these things. It is important, also, to reflect on the things that really set you off. For some, it may be the few choice words people use that can take a situation to the next level. Others may be triggered by actions.

Perhaps a person may get too close and invaded your private space. Maybe it's embarrassment that pushes you to your limit. When you understand this part of yourself, it will help you to recognize these situations, long before they get out of control.

The Bible teaches to walk in love. Jesus walked in love in everything He did and said. It is essential that you take these tests seriously, and try to be as Christ-like as possible. Once you successfully pass one test, it will become easier to identify and pass the next test. When you face a fork-in-the-road moment, consider your options. You can either go left or you can go right, it's all about the choices you make.

You may feel the pressure mount and want to take the easy road, but recognize this is a trick from the devil. Over time, it will require a sacrifice. Lean on your faith. In due time, the signs will become clearer, and the pressure will not be as heavy. Do not fall into the trap or resort to your old self. You were created to conquer. You are victorious! The battle has already been fought and you have already won. Walk in love and you will win every time.

12

SUBWAY TO HEAVEN

MATTHEW 6:18

"That your fasting may not be seen by others but by your Father Who is in secret and your Father Who sees in secret will reward you."

Faith without works is dead. You will have to give up some things in your life, in order to move forward. More specifically, that comfortable lifestyle and those cozy habits you've developed must be eliminated. It's hard to stay in constant prayer for God to move in your life, when there are other areas in your life that need a deep cleanse. Your dependency should be on God, and God alone. It requires much sacrifice and obedience to face your demons. It's time to suffocate and kill what holds you back.

What are you willing to give up so you can walk into the destiny God has designed for your life? Think about all the things you love and need. You must say, "no" to the flesh, and "yes" to God.

LUKE 4:2

"For forty days, being tempted by the devil.
And He ate nothing during those days.
And when they were ended, He was hungry."

TRULY TERRIFIED

For years, I wanted no part of fasting. I was terrified at the thought of going on a fast. It's not like a diet, or a promise I can break the next week. This was an oath made with my Heavenly Father. The process required that I put my faith to work. This thought, alone, scared the crap out of me.

However, in true fashion, God repeatedly showed me others who were fasting around me. For instance, I noticed my friend Eric's music was off, as I rode in the car with him. That was extremely weird to me, because he was a serious music lover. Eric shared with me that he had silenced the music to spend time with God. Wow, now that was deep! I had no idea he had been on a fast.

Then, Joe, my friend and coworker shared with me that he could not view the Facebook post I'd referenced because he was fasting from social media.

Within the same week, I had observed a church member turn down a meal at lunch. He shared with me that he was in the middle of a fast. He would not eat from sunrise to sunset. The sign, had become crystal clear, at this point.

I had received the signs. Each of them sacrificed doing

things they loved the most to get closer to God. They wanted to hear His voice and show God their obedience to His love. They wanted to know Him in a real way. Truly God was telling me something, however, the fear inside of me still screamed, "No way!"

Lowest Low

The devil was hard at work, as he made all hell break loose in my life. My work schedule seemed endless, many times without any days off. I felt empty inside, stuck at this dead end job with no friends. Tears would flow down my face every day with the brutal drive to work. I just did not want to walk into that place. I had even considered the thought of lightly hitting the car in front of mine while stopped at a red light. Not to hurt anyone, of course! I so desperately wanted to call my boss to inform him that I had been in an accident and couldn't make it in. It had gotten that bad!

One day, I slammed right into a brick wall, figuratively speaking. I woke up that morning feeling defeated, made my normal cup of coffee, and pulled out my inspirational books and and began to journal.

After I read, prayed, and praised, I went for my second cup of coffee. Then, the darkness of having to go into work fell upon me. It felt as if this wave had taken over my body, and I could no longer move. "That's it," I told myself. "Today, it ends. I am going to do what I do best: Quit."

The pain I felt was so real, it suffocated me. It was deafening. Life had become normal, and stagnant. But, I am not normal or stagnant. I had known deep down inside, from the time God spoke to me, that I was going somewhere and that big things were in store for me. I knew there had to be more to my life then just to wake up and go to this job everyday. I had so much more to give than that. I fell to the floor, began to weep and cried out to God with all my heart. "God, please, change my circumstances." I was on my knees in prayer with coffee cup in hand. I truly surrendered my all to Christ.

Please picture this: I was in my pajamas, literally rocking back and forth on the floor like a crazy person. I had made the ugliest face known to man, as I screamed out to God. This was my truth. This was my full and complete surrender. But, for some strange reason, I would not let go of my coffee cup. I noticed the tan mug in my hand, one of my favorites, was still filled halfway with coffee.

It was at that moment, I realized it was time to let go. I had asked God for so many things. I craved them, and begged God to save me. However, love is an action word. If I wanted a gateway to God's heart, I needed to act. I wanted to show God that I loved Him and surrendered to Him. The very next day, I began my first fast. "Goodbye coffee, see you in 40 long days!"

MATTHEW 9:14-15

"One day the disciples of John the Baptist
came to Jesus and asked him, "Why don't your
disciples fast like we do and the Pharisees
do?" Jesus replied, "Do wedding guests mourn

> while celebrating with the groom? Of course not. But someday the groom will be taken away from them, and then they will fast."

Why Coffee?

It may seem small to you, but coffee was my happy place. It was my everyday ritual. Living was my darkness. Coffee was my one piece of light. I looked forward to it, daily. I'd get excited as it brewed in the morning. It was as if a cup of coffee and my Bible went hand-in-hand. They fit perfectly together.

When I reported, and needed a hint of goodness in my life, I would run to Starbucks for my peace. It was the one thing that could make me smile after a long, tumultuous day. I couldn't fall asleep, because I was too excited about my anticipated, early morning coffee experience. I loved the sweet, aroma of coffee. The intoxicated smell gently awakened me, and helped jumpstart my day. This is what coffee symbolized for me. It was my "Go to." It's almost like it had taken the place of God, in some strange way. God wanted me to put Him first, for Him to become my "Go to."

Let the Fasting Begin

I wanted God to move in my life. I wanted Him to take the wheel of the car and drive. I needed to surrender all. I was ready to fast. I spoke to God and connected with Him, in a way I never had before. It was difficult to not wake up to my favorite cup of coffee. When it was time to dive into my morning meditation, and I didn't have any coffee to accompany the routine, I had to pray.

When I had a bad day at work, and needed a tasty, pick-me-up cup of coffee, I had to pray. My relationship with God grew tremendously as I replaced my coffee with prayer. When I tried to cut back on my coffee intake years prior, it left me with excruciating caffeine headaches. I'd anticipated the same, painful, caffeine withdrawals with this fast, but it never happened. For 40 days, I prayed every time I got weak. In the Bible, Jesus shows us how to remain strong and speak to God in a fast.

Matthew 4:1-11

"Then Jesus was led by the Spirit into the wilderness to be tempted by the devil. After fasting forty days and forty nights, He was hungry. The tempter came to Him and said, "If you are the Son of God, tell these stones to become bread." Jesus answered, "It is written: 'Man shall not live on bread alone, but on every word that comes from the mouth of God.' Then the devil took Him to the holy city and had Him stand on the highest point of the temple. 'If You are the Son of God,' He said, 'throw Yourself down. For it is written: He will command His angels concerning You, and they will lift You up in their hands, so that You will not strike your foot against a stone.' Jesus

> answered him, 'it is also written: 'Do not put the Lord Your God to the test.' Again, the devil took Him to a very high mountain and showed Him all the kingdoms of the world and their splendor. 'All this I will give You,' he said, 'if You will bow down and worship me.' Jesus said to him, 'Away from Me, Satan! For it is written: 'Worship the Lord your God, and serve Him only.' Then the devil left Him, and angels came and attended Him."

Gets Easier

In the beginning, there were times of weakness. I call them "trigger moments." When I'd see people sip from a Starbucks cup, I'd feel weak. My mind would go straight to the calendar, to see how much longer I had to be on the fast. Each time, I would refocus my fast on God, and lean on Him for strength.

Throughout the course of the fast, I began to grow stronger in my spirit, which brought me closer to God. I got so strong until I was able to actually attend meetings held in different Starbucks locations. The fast renewed my spirit. I surrendered my doubts and fears, and my spirit was able to drink from the fountain of my love for God. I felt ready for anything. Fasting made me come alive for Jesus!

I Did It, So Can You

Essentially, my own fears caused me to prolong in darkness. I believe it was my fast that showed God I was completely ready to change. Now, I have a renewed and strengthened spirit. Today, I fast often. If there is weakness over an area in my life, I fast. I am on a fast write now as I write this to you.

Give the spirit within you the power and authority to move in your life. Do not be scared. You will find yourself in the same place for the next 20 years, if you allow fear to rule you. Joel Osteen said it perfectly, "Your destiny is too great, your assignment too important, your time too valuable. Do not let fear intimidate you." I did it, so can you.

FAST

Go on a sincere fast. Think of what you absolutely love; then, make the choice to give it to God. Only you know what it is. I've seen some people do simple fasts. For example, you may choose to fast from exercising when, let's face it, you hate exercising. Where's the sacrifice? If you make it easy for yourself, then you've erased the true meaning of a fast, which is to rely on God's strength.

When you fast, it's an action of obedience to God. If you truly want to refresh your spirit, you must be serious. If you eliminate certain foods from your diet, make no mistake your body will know it. You will suffer a shock from the with-drawals. You will notice people around you eating what you've chosen to give up. They may even offer it to you.

You may be sitting in traffic and see the person in the car next to you eating what you can't. You might see it on television commercials and hear about it on the radio. It might be talked about on conference calls, and written about all over social media. Everywhere you turn, the devil will try to break you down. He does not want your prayers to make it to God. Resist the devil. You must say, "No" to the flesh and "Yes" to God.

JAMES 4:7

"Submit yourselves therefore to God. Resist the devil, and he will flee from you."

When you drive to work, you may hit traffic, road blocks, construction, and stop signs that prolong your journey, to your final destination. I see fasting as a subway train directly to God's heart. You have a prayer that you want to take directly to God. Instead of taking the long route, jump on the subway train to heaven. There are no lights to stop this train. There's no engine failure, no accidents, or roadblocks to stop the flow of traffic. Once you sit, with prayer in hand, the train takes off at full speed, next stop - God.

If you need a change in your life, you will be required to make even bigger sacrifices. You may want your children to get off drugs, or connect with the father you never met. You may have dreamed to one-day walk across the stage to receive your bachelors, masters or even your doctorate degree. These may appear as impossible feats, but God will make the impossible possible.

You have to work for it. You have to hurt for it. Stand on your faith, and let God show you His hand. Go on your first fast. Give it up to God for 40 days, and watch the changes happen in your life. Get on this subway train to Heaven with me. A seat has been saved, just for you!

Daniel 9:3

"And I set my face unto the Lord God,
to seek by prayer and supplications, with
fasting, and sackcloth, and ashes."

13

CLEAN HOUSE

1 Peter 5: 6-8

"Humble yourselves, therefore, under God's mighty hand, that He may lift you up in due time. Cast all your anxiety on Him because He cares for you. Be self-controlled and alert. Your enemy the devil prowls around like a roaring lion looking for someone to devour."

The way your life unfolds is part of God's plan. Worry, on the other hand, is a sign of the devil's stronghold over you. It's a hell of mind-battling woes, that only you create for yourself. "I just got laid off. I can't afford these bills. How am I going to raise these children on my own? How can I walk away from this job that I hate?"

A state of "worry" is when you try to control the uncontrollable. Constant negativity will seep into your soul and defeat you. It will ultimately create distance between you and God. Allow God to be in full control of your life. His will is always better than ourselves.

PHILIPPIANS 4:6-7

"Do not be anxious about anything, but
in everything, by prayer and petition, with
thanksgiving, present your requests to God.
And the peace of God, which transcends
all understanding, will guard your hearts
and your minds in Christ Jesus."

It was Lent season, which marked the start of a new 40 day fast. However, I had just gotten off my first fast and was not excited to dive into another one so soon. I was unsure of my level of strength. I began to pray. Then, boom! It hit me. My next fast would consist of living worry free for 40 days.

THE DEVIL CREEPS

The devil is sneaky. He creeps around you all day. He lurks. He waits patiently. He laughs at you, every time you let him in. All he can do is whisper thoughts to you. However, his thoughts are to steal, kill, and destroy. If these thoughts of worry, fear, and doubt are let in, they will ultimately kill you.

JOHN 10:10

"The thief comes only to steal and kill and
destroy. I came that they may
have life and have it abundantly."

24/7 Protection

I began to treat my mind as an actual house that needed 24/7 protection. As negative thoughts lurked around my home, I developed a full-time job to lock them out. Philippians 4:8 states, "An idle mind is a devil's playground." I knew I needed to stay protected. Every negative thought that snuck in, I knew was sent by the devil to destroy me. I needed to recognize it as that.

The devil was a real threat to my life. If I blinked my eyes, I saw anxiousness creep in through a cracked window. Fear had the audacity to ring the doorbell, and boldly walk in through the front door. I was under constant attack. This was definitely spiritual warfare. I had to double, and triple check my locks on a consistent basis. If a negative thought ever got by me, I needed to sweep it right out the back door.

"You can't stay here, devil." No thoughts of this nature could stay in my home. Not even for a second. It would only be a matter of time before friends like worry, doubt, excuses, and confusion would sneak in, too.

The key is to understand negative thoughts always linger. Establish peace within yourself, as you recognize you cannot erase them. They will always be present. Your only job is to "clean house." Remove these thoughts that have accumulated like dust. It's time to issue an eviction notice.

Proverbs 4:23

"Keep thy heart with all diligence; for out of it are the issues of life".

Weapons of War

Another weapon to help fight and win the war on worry is to keep scriptures close to your heart. As I continued my fast, I would recite scriptures that spoke to my circumstances, like Philippians 4:13, "I can do all things through Christ who strengthens me." This was my favorite scripture. Any time a thought of worry tried to ooze into my mind, I would boomerang it with this scripture. For the easiest and most powerful weapon during spiritual warfare, simply, say the name Jesus. Jeremiah 10:6 says, "There's power in His name."

After a week of beating down worry, I no longer struggled with it. I would hear the attempts loud and clear, like a security alarm went off. I would immediately shoot it down and kill that thought. I decided to take my "no-worry" fast, to limitless possibility. I didn't stop after the 40 days, as planned. I still live worry-free, to this day.

As a faith believer, your current state will not always be your tomorrow. Live with expectancy in your heart that God is in control. Instead of worry, focus all your thoughts and energy on God. You either believe in God, or you don't. You either stand on Faith, or you allow worry to govern you. God takes pleasure every time His children overcome the devil's attempts. Continue to boldly praise His name, in the midst of the storm. You are Uniquely Qualified with a suited armor, to win the war on worry.

Matthew 14:30

"But when he saw the wind, he was afraid and,
beginning to sink, cried out, 'Lord save me'."

MAKE IT YOUR MISSION

The devil does not want you to remember scripture. He will use every tactic in the world, to keep you away from God. He will trick you to never want to open the Bible. 2 Corinthians 10: 4 says, "For the weapons of our warfare are not of the flesh but have divine power to destroy strongholds." You may easily remember catchy songs on the radio, but the devil will make you draw a blank every time you try to recite a scripture. The devil cannot have you. Your next activity is solely dedicated to learning scriptures.

Start today. Try your best to learn scriptures. When you have a horrible day and everything goes wrong, you will then have God's word to speak life over your situation. Meditate on these scriptures. Murmur the powerful words. Use scriptures when you pray. Fill up your life with His word. Any area of your life that is not the Lord's is overtaken by the devil.

The first scripture I imprinted on my heart was Hebrews 11:1, "Faith is the substance of all things hoped for, the evidence of things not seen." It took forever to remember this one scripture, but I made it my mission. I finally learned by setting alarms.

Time ever changes. It's all around us, and never stops. Time is God's protection over our lives. Let's use time to help us learn His word. Pick a time of the day. Any time will do. Set your alarm clock for whatever time you choose. When the alarm goes off, take time to spend a couple minutes to learn a new scripture.

For example, at 11:10am I recounted Hebrews 11:10 scripture. Use the alarm on your cell phone, since it's always by your side.

I also recommend you use the notepad in your phone to store your scriptures. When you spend time alone with God, beautiful scriptures will jump out and speak to your spirit. Write them down and save them, so you can always reference them.

When your alarm clock alerts you at your designated time, no matter what you are doing at that time, you owe it to yourself to stop, open up these scriptures; and give your mind a refresher. This daily practice will give you the power you'll need to imprint powerful scriptures on your heart. These scriptures form mighty weapons and armor to handle any and all of life's battles.

14

FORGIVENESS

2 Chronicles 7:14

"If My people, who are called by My name, will humble themselves and pray and seek My face and turn from their wicked ways, then I will hear from Heaven, and I will forgive their sin and heal their land."

One of the biggest obstacles I have ever had to face in my life was when I had to walk away from a dear friend, Raquel. We did everything together. We finished each other's thoughts. I was the 'yin' to her 'yang'. When Raquel came up with schemes and pranks, it was my job to craft ways to pull them off. She never left me alone, and would put herself at risk to make sure I was safe, always.

I could never go anywhere without someone asking where Raquel was. We were inseparable. We ignited something in each other. I was fearless with her. We were unbroken, yet reckless and untouchable. As little kids, I remember her mom telling us to hold on to our friendship, as we grew older. We were terrified at the thought, and made a vow to always be there for each other. Times have since changed.

One day, we were forced to face the heat. We were no good for each other. Our season had ended. We brought out ugly behavior in each other, which caused our friendship to grow sour. Love turned to jealousy and hate. For many years, we stopped speaking to each other. Raquel moved on with her life; got married, and had children. I moved on with mine.

Her life flourished, as I missed out on all the milestones we dreamed about as kids. There was a dark space inside of me. Even still, I could not let go of her, as my friend. I was angry at how our relationship had ended. We were no longer friends, and I was no longer able to lean on my better half. Raquel was gone. Anger took her place.

> "You are responsible for your life. You can't keep blaming somebody else for your dysfunction. Life is really about moving on."
>
> Oprah Winfrey

The Time is Now

As embarrassed as I felt and as shameful as it was, I had to release myself of that burden. I had to reach out to her, in hopes that she would receive my apology. Seven years later, I found Raquel on social media. I inboxed her, and wondered if she even checked her messages. I was amazed when she replied. She was shocked, but open to meet with me. I took a drive back to my hometown of Hampton, VA. The whole day, I was filled with nerves. I stayed in constant prayer, in hopes of receiving love from her. I did not want to relive past hurt.

However, I needed to look Raquel in her eyes, so I could gracefully move forward. We chose a random place to meet, but God revealed our reunion to me in a dream the night before. In the dream, He showed us meeting at a nearby Ruby Tuesday. It was a place she used to work as a teenager, and a location I used to pass regularly when I lived in Hampton. Right before our scheduled time to meet, she changed locations to that Ruby Tuesday. How crazy! That was confirmation.

I walked through the doors and looked around the room. I immediately spotted her. She was at a booth, by herself. She sat up straight, stone faced, and very cold. Her demeanor was stiff. I could tell Raquel was unsure of what to say, or why she even accepted my invitation. But, I remembered the real her. I needed to look past her tough exterior. I knew her heart was still in it, as was mine.

I took a seat across from her, in the booth. No small talk was required; we had too much history for that. God took over. I had driven seven hours from Charlotte, to sit down, across from my childhood sister, to apologize for breaking all of our promises. Yes, circumstances had changed in our lives. I'd missed out on her life, and she had missed out on mine. I was sorry she had to do it without me. Every minute that passed, we loosened our grip. Anger lost out to love. Our seasons had changed.

However, I needed to come face-to-face with my past. I was in a prison of unforgiveness. I had to surrender my pride, ego, and faults for my vulnerability to be set free. After seven years, our walls came down; and we laughed together for the first time. Forgiveness had freed us.

"Forgiveness is a reflection of loving yourself enough to move on."

DR. STEVE MARABOLI

DROP IT ALL

In order to move forward in life and surrender, you must learn to let it all go. That means everything. Loosen the death-grip. Don't hold on to anger. It will ultimately destroy you. The devil will use past hurt to keep you stagnant in your faith journey. I was unable to truly move forward in my life, because I held onto resentment. It seemed like the hardest thing to do was to simply let go. Over time, Raquel and I slowly got back to a place of peace and friendship.

Today, I smile at the thought of her. No one in my life will ever take her place. Raquel was my better half, my best friend. Only she holds all of the memories of our childhood. I could never explain to anyone what we did, and what we shared. Not even my husband could be brought up to speed. I will always love her and respect the friendship we shared. It's an understanding that no one could ever take the other's place. Not now. Not ever. This is what it means to surrender all.

LOOK FOR THE "WE"

Friends come and go. Some leave an imprint on your life, while others are only meant to be there for a season. Childhood friends do not characterize lifelong friends. It simply means they knew you, "when." New friends do not mean they can't become the best of friends. Time does not make a friend. It's their heart, character, values, and how they treat you, that make them a friend. Some friendships are instantaneous, and last forever.

Other friendships may take a little longer to grow. I've said before, we are not meant to do life alone. In this activity, I encourage you to look for the "we." What I mean is, look for the person who says, "Your problems are my problems. Your ups are my ups, and your downs are mine, as well." Look for the person who treats you better than they treat themselves.

Look for people who are loyal, who care, and have a big heart. Look for people who love, give, respect, and most importantly, cherish every second with you. A beautiful friendship is one which encourages the differences shared, with no want to change a single one of them.

Adrienne Campbell is that friend to me. When I talk to her, she says, "This is how we will get through this. This is what we can do to overcome. Here's where we need to start." No matter where I am in life, she stops right where she is; listens, and treats my every situation like it's her own. I encourage you to look for the "We" in your life. It may be someone you've known forever. It may be someone you just met. Time does not signify true friendship. The person does.

"I've learned that people will forget what you said, people will forget what you did, but people will never forget how you made them feel."

MAYA ANGELOU

15

BECOME THE BLESSING

CORINTHIANS 9:7

"Each one must do just as he has purposed in his heart, not grudgingly or under compulsion, for God loves a cheerful giver. And God is able to make all grace abound to you, so that always having all sufficiency in everything; you may have abundance for every good deed."

Give at the expense of yourself, no matter the cost. The Bible says in Luke 6:38, "Give, and it shall be given unto you; good measure, pressed down, and shaken together, and running over, shall men give into your bosom. For with the same measure that ye mete withal it shall be measured to you again." When you look down at what you have, and give sacrificially, a spiritual awakening takes place. There is a sense of worth and establishment, in the separation of what is yours, and what belongs to others. The Bible encourages bold and radical faith, by giving from your heart.

Growing up, I wore the hat of selfishness. I felt that I worked hard to earn these things, and others should, too. Raquel, who I shared with you in the previous chapter should have been able to come to me for anything, but no, she would run to others when in need. She said I never helped her. My excuse, it was hard to constantly bail her out of what I perceived as repeated, bad decisions. I felt that she blew her money on meaningless things, while I sacrificed and saved. I could not keep bailing her out, so I would give her anything. This pushed her to go to others for help.

I've since learned, giving neither holds judgment nor has boundaries. It's solely about the blessing. That is the only rule.

I once heard my preacher, the late Bishop Phillip M. Davis, go deep into the art of giving. He said, "Until we voluntarily do for someone else, so much that we suffer with them, we haven't truly learned what it means to give of ourselves." That's what Jesus did for us. God gave His only begotten Son to walk with us, suffer with us, and to die at the expense of our sins. We are not worthy of Him, but He still made the ultimate sacrifice to us, in His giving.

PHILIPPIANS 3:7

"I once thought these things were valuable,
but now I consider them worthless
because of what Christ has done."

Art of Giving

When you walk in a giving spirit, you will overflow with amazement and pure gratitude. Not only will you make someone else's day, a shower of blessing will fall upon your heart, as well. When you invest in someone else's happiness, you will feel a tingle that makes you smile inside. Proverbs 19:17 says, "If you help the poor, you're lending to the Lord- and He will repay you!" How amazing! The planted seed of one person's giving nature has now sprouted two blessings.

"The meaning of life is to find your gift.
The purpose of life is to give it away."

William Shakespeare

Giving comes in a variety of ways. There are tangible and intangible forms of giving. Materialistic gifts like clothes, jewelry, and shoes may come easy for some. However, intangible gifts do not cost anything. The possibilities are endless. For instance, you can truly change someone's day with the gift of your smile. Just think. A stranger walks by you in the store, however, you don't know they've had a bad day. Send them a genuine smile. That one act, alone, may have brought a smile to their face and changed the rest of their day. Never underestimate the value of a smile. You have the power and the ability to create change. Giving mirrors your heart. What's inside of yours?

A Tiny, Massive Gift

My girlfriend Danielle called to share how unhappy she had been and that she felt like she could barely hold on. I knew this was a "friend moment" where I needed to drop everything and just be with her. I invited her on a nature walk. I wanted Danielle to slow down for a second and take in the beauty that surrounded her. It was not my idea; God's actually. He had given me an assignment. God wanted to use me to help open her eyes.

I planned to arrive early. Anyone who knows me, knows I'm never on time. Part of me wanted to buy her a gift, but if I stopped I would've definitely been late. Then, I received a text from her that said she would be 10 minutes late. This was the sign I had waited for. I immediately took the next exit, and parked in front of a Christian book store.

God placed on my heart to get her a copy of Sarah Young's "Jesus Calling," a daily devotional. I believed this devotional would empower and strengthen her love for Christ. I arrived at our meeting place, with her gift in hand. We opened it up, and read the devotional for that morning. That daily devotional cost little to no money, but it truly blessed her.

The next week, she shared that not only did she read it each morning, but her boyfriend and his best friend read it as well. God used me to simply plant a seed in their lives. All I had to do was listen to God's assignment, say "Yes," and allow God to do the rest.

Even in your darkness, God will use you for His divine

purpose. You may suffer with depression, anxiety, and doubt. You may feel that you are not qualified to help others, since you are in the storm of your life. But, this is not true. God can still use you, for His good. You have already been Uniquely Qualified for the assignment. There is nothing that you can't do without God. Answer every assignment God places in your life. It will bless others, as well as you.

Matthew 5:16

"Let your light shine before men, that
they may see your good works, and glorify
your Father which is in Heaven."

Ssshhhh God is Talking

Before God removed years of dissatisfaction from my life, my misery had company. Danielle and I often rambled a long list of complaints while at work. It's like we almost competed to see who had it the worse. I was on the verge of quitting; questioned my financial stability; and was unsure of what career move to make, next. Her story was was the exact same.

On this particular day, I could barely scrape up the strength for myself, let alone comfort anyone else. It was a moment I will never forget. I watched Danielle speak and could see her lips move, but could no longer hear her voice. It felt as though time slowed down. I was unable to move, or speak.

God was talking to me. Some would describe this as an

outer-body experience. His loud whisper jolted me to my core. "I hear you ask for blessings, but, I want you to be the blessing," are the words God spoke. I immediately shared the message with Danielle, and watched her run straight to the computer. Her demeanor went from despair to pure joy. This was her moment of clarity and a confirmation she had waited for. She began to research an idea that had been on her heart all day: Feeding the hungry. On that evening, Hashtag Lunchbag Charlotte was born.

#LunchBagCLT

Hashtag Lunchbag is a nonprofit, grassroots movement based out of a number of U.S. cities. Complete strangers join together to serve homeless populations with lunch bags. Not only do the bags have food in them, but they also contain love notes of inspiration. Four days after that defining moment with God, we launched the first event in Charlotte. We had 12 volunteers. It was midnight on a Friday, and we made sandwiches. There were prep stations set up to pack the lunch bags. Another designated station wrote the love notes. We had a hand-written sign I will never forget. It read: "Hashtag Lunchbag Charlotte." This signified that we were ready to feed souls.

The next morning, we all met up at 8am to hand out the lunch bags. We traveled to the areas where the need was great. Many people smiled and said, "God bless you." We walked for hours, until the last bag was given away. That was a day we will all remember. We could have been anywhere else, at that time.

Instead, together, we decided it was more important to wake up early and serve our community. It was a rewarding experience, filled with such fulfillment. We wanted to keep the momentum going. We decided to do Hashtag Lunchbag Charlotte once a month, every month. To this day, we have never missed one. A day of complaining amongst two girlfriends had given hope.

MATTHEW 25:35

"For I was hungry, and you fed me. I was thirsty,
and you gave me a drink. I was a stranger,
and you invited me into your home."

One cold winter, two ladies knitted wool hats to go into each bag. I remember as I drove through Uptown Charlotte, I saw so many people on the street with those hats on. It felt great to know we had made a difference. I will always be grateful for the day our focused changed. Hashtag Lunchbag Charlotte continues to bring the community together, with the sole purpose of giving back. This is a true piece of happiness, only achieved when you do for someone else, knowing they're unable to repay you.

We received our message from God. It's time for you to hone in on yours! Silence the noise around you, including your own words and thoughts. Many times, you are so busy talking that you fill the air around you with dead words. This ultimately will dig you deeper into your darkness. Learn to bask in the stillness of God's presence. He knows your troubles. He knows your desires. Let Him lead you. Allow God's voice to overpower yours.

"You get the best out of others when
you give the best of yourself."

HARVET S. FIRESTONE

BLESSING BAGS

As I cleaned out my garage one day, I found all sorts of cool stuff. I no longer wanted or needed them, so I began to think of how I could give them away. I started to craft these blessing bags to give away to people who live on the street. I started to build these bags for men and women. The women's bags had nail polish and body wash I had collected, from different hotels I'd stayed in. I also put cute t-shirts, collected from random events, in them. I then looked around my house for items to place in the bags, to make them special.

I did the same thing for the men's bags. I came across a huge box of cologne and body wash. I started to get excited! This was stuff that I would ultimately have thrown away. Instead, I began to build blessing bags that would completely make someone else's day. As I placed all the bags in my trunk, I prayed for God to lead me to His people.

As I left for work that day, I jumped on a conference call. The call was so in-depth, that I literally drove right past Subway, which was where I had wanted to eat for lunch. Once I got off the phone, I saw another Subway pop up on the very next interstate sign, so I took it. I started to thank God as he took me down that street.

When I pulled up, to the restaurant, I immediately saw a man on the side of the street. When I walked in, God began to speak to me. I got excited! Yes, God was using me. I stood in line and ordered my meal. I also got a separate meal for the man I'd seen.

When I walked to my car, I asked him to join me. He hesitated and asked if I was sure. I knew this was what I was supposed to do. As other men on their lunch breaks walked to their cars; they stared at us in shock. I handed him his lunch and a blessing bag that I had made earlier that day. He began to cry tears of gratefulness.

For this exercise, you need to keep the trunk of your car filled with blessing bags. Therefore, you will always have them on hand when you see someone who is in need. Go to your junk drawer. Walk into your garage or closet space and take a deep breath. You hold special treasures in these spaces that can be a blessing to others. All you need to do is organize it. Create blessing bags from things you no longer use.

For example, when you attend different events, you will typically receive gift bags. Once you go through it all, there's probably only one or two items you want, or can use. Don't throw anything away. Find creative ways to fill bags with items others may need. Build your blessing bags today!

16

GRATEFULNESS

2 CORINTHIANS 9:11

"Thus you will be enriched in all things and in every way, so that you can be generous, and your generosity, as it is administered by us will bring forth thanksgiving to God."

Some of us believe we were dealt a bad hand from the time we were born. Our family situations may have been bad from day one. Some of those parental bonds may be nonexistent, to this day. The harsh reality is we are not all granted the same privileges. This can be hard to deal with, and sometimes perceived as blatantly unfair. Do not compare your life to someone else's. Comparison is the thief of happiness. The hand you were dealt was Uniquely orchestrated for you, and you alone. Your trials and tribulations were meant to teach you great lessons. Those tough moments were meant to shape you and mold you. Other people's lessons were meant to shape them. God's word holds true. Jeremiah 29:11 reads, "For I know the plans I have for you," says the Lord. "They are plans for good and not for disaster, to give you a future and a hope."

"We either make ourselves miserable, or we make ourselves strong. The amount of work is the same."

Carlos Castaneda

A Waiting Child's Story

At the TV station, I cover a feature segment called, "Waiting Child." The children we spotlight in these stories live with foster families, in hopes of permanent adoption. I spend the day with them, and get to know them, personally. I, then, create the best story that represents who they are, to encourage adoption.

I listen as they tell their stories. At times, I've felt absolutely heartbroken. These kids have faced some of life's hardest lessons, yet some of them are only in elementary school. They have no mom. They have no dad. If they do have parents, perhaps the parents are on drugs, or have hurt the child in unimaginable ways.

The kids can sometimes be uprooted between numerous schools, cities, and states. Several kids have been moved from as many as 14+ different homes. Some kids have said all they want for Christmas is a mom. Many of the children I've spent time with believe a family solely provides things like food, clothes, and a roof.

They have no idea that a family also loves, nourishes,

cares, and supports, forever. I then realized that the constant thread that runs through each story is: They simply want someone to love them.

One 14-year-old, in particular, taught me so much about life, in just 30 minutes. He said, "What family would want me if I was sad, mad, and depressed all the time? So, I have to smile." Just like every child I feature, he refuses to let the bad things in his life hold him back. We all can learn from a waiting child.

"Choose one thing that you are grateful for and make it your mantra for today."

LUCY MCDONALD

TRAGIC BLESSING

Earlier in the book, I asked you to think of the worst thing that has ever happened to you. Now ask yourself: Can you find gratefulness in it? This might be tough, dependent upon the circumstance and length of time since it's occurred. If you struggle, this may be an indication that you have not yet released it to God. I urge you not to do this alone. Allow for God to ease your hurt and pain.

PSALM 55:22

"Cast your cares on the Lord and He will sustain you; He will never let the righteous be shaken."

In life, there are joys and there are pains. We must endure them both. When life hits you with pain, even if it takes years to find peace, do not let it suffocate you. God rains down blessings, daily. Open your heart and your spirit to receive them, even if it hurts. Free yourself from the pain. Remember some pains are disguised as blessings.

Let's consider a mother's loss of her child. I reference this example, because I believe this has to be one of the worst tragedies in the entire universe. How in the world can there be gratefulness in this, you may ask? I pray, if ever faced with such a situation, that I can forgive everyone involved, this includes myself and God.

I also pray for a thankful spirit, to be able to say to God, "Thank You. You have allowed me to be the mother of Your sweet, precious angel. Thank You, God. You allowed me to raise and love Your little angel. I now know this child was never mine, only Yours. I thank You for Your trust in me, as I raised up Your child."

Romans 8:28

"And we know that God causes everything to work together for the good of those who Love God and are called according to His purpose for them."

MIND, BODY & SOUL

When on the road to true spiritual rejuvenation, the entire body needs to be balanced. In addition to diving in the word, prayer, and fasting, your physical body needs work, as well. Just as you strengthen your spirit, you need to work your physical body, also. Your body's a temple and should be physically, mentally and spiritually nourished.

One summer, me and my girlfriend Audrina, along with a few other friends started a workout group, called "Field at 9." At 9am, hence the name, we would meet at an open field to work out. We had such a great time! It's always best to have a friend, or a team of people to work out with. They hold you accountable and push you at your weakest moment. We took turns as we called out different workouts. This would add a fresh new spin to each session.

What made our workout Unique was our fellowship and prayer sessions that followed each workout. Many times, we would leave the field; go make our healthy green shakes, and then have impromptu Bible studies on the patio in the back yard.

Wow, look at God! Before officially starting the day, our physical bodies were strengthened, and we spent valuable time with God. When your mind, body, and soul are strengthened daily, your spirit stays refreshed.

You develop energy when you work out. I suggest you work out, even when you feel tired. You can easily find a workout class or a gym to join. I also suggest a fun outdoor activity or group to join, where there's lots of physical movement. If you can still find excuses with all of these, then get to a free walking trail!

For example, my mom's form of exercise is to take long walks. It started with 15-minute increments. Today, she strives to hit 20,000 steps, daily. She also says the walks have become spiritual sessions with God. She tells me when she walks, God talks to her and feeds her soul.

Include physical movement in your life. You may not know this, but when you strengthen your physical muscles, you also develop endorphins in your blood which kick-start thoughts in your mind. If you don't believe me, I dare you to try it, today!

17

ANSWER THE CALLING

2 PETER 1:10-11

"Therefore, brothers, be all the more diligent to make your calling and election sure, for if you practice these qualities you will never fall. For in this way there will be richly provided for you an entrance into the eternal kingdom of our Lord and Savior Jesus Christ."

Tim, the General Manager of the news station called me into his office, for a meeting. It was good news, I guess. Tim had offered me a promotion at the TV station. "Who, me?" I was confused. I guess Kevin, my immediate News Director never shared my unhappiness with him.

Any sane person would have been thrilled to hear that kind of news. I was grateful for the opportunity, but unsure I wanted to move up within that company. Especially, since I had been depressed, for so long.

This was considered an opportunity of a lifetime. It was the big break I'd waited for. That's what the company thought, anyways. That promotion would come with a hefty salary increase, more exposure, and better hours.

However, I would still do the same things that had brought me so much misery. I talked it over with my family and close friends, eager to get their advice. They entertained the thought, and believed the bigger platform would allow me to serve God, in a larger capacity. And, when they heard how much money I would make, they really urged me to accept the promotion.

For me, the idea to accept the promotion did not sit well, nor did it fall in line with my spirit. I felt an uneasy tug in the pit of my stomach. All of the circumstances appeared to be great. But, could I really put a price tag on my peace and happiness?

"Peace at any cost is no peace, at all."

Dr. Phil

Follow the Tugs

There are times in our life when circumstances do not sit right in our stomach. These moments will rock us to the core. We may fool ourselves and make excuses, but we can't hide from the uneasiness. When we feel unsettled, it is the Holy Spirit's attempts to guide us away from unforeseen dangers. Our job is to slow down and take notice to the message, which awaits to be received.

We must make ourselves available to listen, and allow the Holy Spirit to rescue us. The Holy Spirit will guide every area of our life. Activate it. If we attempt to move forward, as we ignore God's signals, we will eventually get burned. Most of us often do.

Your decision to read this book was not an accident. You may be in a storm of your life right now, due to a rushed decision and non-adherence to the guidance of your Holy Spirit. Things could've been different, if only you had listened to the still, small, precious whispers from within.

My best advice: Follow the tugs. Listen to your Holy Spirit. Wait on God's confirmation.

One week after I met with my General Manager, I made the life-changing decision to silence the Holy Spirit. I had planned to accept the offer. It made logical sense, right? Yes, I would still be unhappy, but I would make more money, so I needed to do it. I thought it would be dumb of me, if I didn't take the job. Tim and I were long overdue to meet, after a series of unexpected cancellations. Little occurrences continued to pop up, and force us to reschedule. Two weeks had passed. The meeting was pushed back three different times, which gave God ample time to tug on my spirit.

The day finally presented itself. I jumped in the shower and immediately began to fall sick. I felt nauseous. I wrote it off, because I had lots to get done that day. Plus, there was no way we could push back this very important meeting, again.

I could barely get dressed. I tried to throw on some makeup. I still pushed myself past the sweat that dripped from my forehead.

My upset stomach continued to churn. I had no idea what was going on with my body. That sickness came out of nowhere. I jumped in the car and could barely see. My vision was blurred. My hands shook, as though I had a bad nervous condition. "What the heck?" I thought. This was unlike me to be nervous for a meeting. I couldn't figure out what the trigger was. I started my drive into work. Halfway through my route, I began to speak to God. I asked the one question that I was most scared to hear Him answer: "God, do you want me to take this job?"

I started to envision walking away from my job. Instantly, insurmountable peace took over my body. I felt a sense of peace like I had never fully been able to grasp. God's answer was so sound, that I almost didn't recognize it. God's perfect plan for me did not include this job promotion.

As soon as I followed the tug of the Holy Spirit, my sickness left. I walked into the meeting, with supreme confidence. I thanked Tim for the consideration. I then explained to him that God had a calling on my life. He immediately looked up at me, stunned. As he moved away from his computer, he began to share part of his story with me.

Tim told me that God had called him, years ago. He explained that fear held him back, so he never answered the call. To my surprise, I was not fired on the spot, as I expressed my feelings. I was actually embraced. My boss congratulated me for being strong enough to hear the whispers of the Lord, and for being obedient to His call.

He then pulled up my contract to see how much longer I had left with the company. I felt God's presence in the room. Everything changed, at that moment. I was freed. God made what seemed impossible become completely possible, within minutes. Instead of being told I had to fulfill the remainder of my contract, Tim told me he would grant my wish and let me break it. This is unheard of.

In addition, he asked me if I would be willing to stay a couple months until they could find a replacement. My boss still granted me the raise, anyways. He shared with me that, if I ever wanted to come back to the station I could. He also asked if I would be interested in assisting the station as a freelancer, which I eagerly obliged. My boss explained to me that he would not want to stand in the way of what God had placed in my heart, and would help in any way that he could. When God's favor rains, it pours!

It Actually Happened

I walked into the dressing room after the meeting to prepare for the next show. I was completely shocked! Nothing happened the way I had expected it to. He didn't get angry. He didn't fire me; and, no, he didn't yell. My boss congratulated me for answering God's call. Then, I sat back and watched God give abundantly more than I ever asked for. I was granted the raise and given the purpose-filled community stories I had always wanted to do.

I was given a cushion of six months to build a new career plan. I was also given the opportunity to continue on-air duties, as an on-call reporter. I was given the green light to come back, if I needed to. For the first time, I could see the light at the end of the tunnel. I could breathe. God has answered my long-awaited prayer. God showed up in a mighty way. I began to pray as gratefulness overflowed from my soul.

When there are decisions that need to be made in your life, take them to God. Slow down your life to a still, quiet place, where you can hear and feel the tugs of the Holy Spirit. As a result, God will show up and guide your steps. The devil's evil schemes, whispers of doubt, and worry, will trick you to believe you should make a certain decision, due to money and opportunity.

The devil will also disguise his plan as he creates urgency for rushed decisions. Don't fall for it. Even though God's way may look blurred and not make complete sense, it will guarantee peace and joy. Get out of your comfort zone, and rely solely on your faith and trust in God.

My Last Day

My contract with that station simulated a mountain in my life. I felt like I was in prison. I was stuck in stagnation. God moved that mountain. On my last full day, I shared my testimony multiple times on-air, during the morning show. I spoke of my love for God, and shared my desire to live purposeful.

Please, tell me. How unheard of was is it to hear someone speak of God on a news broadcast? I thought people would turn the channel in disgust, and hate me as I spoke about my faith walk.

To my surprise, people celebrated with me. I began to walk in my peace. I did not hold back. I received emails from pastors who asked me to speak in front of their congregation. I had viewers write in and ask how they, too, could serve God. People all around the community told me how refreshing it was to see someone walk away from a career, to do God's work.

Little did I know, the seed I had planted, as I shared my testimony on TV, would spark a movement within so many others. God had used me, and it felt great. This was the feeling I had searched for. That was what I'd been called to do. That was, indeed, my purpose. I am Uniquely Qualified. I began to walk in my destiny. When I drove away from the station that morning, I tasted freedom for the first time.

"Sometimes there is no next time, no time-outs,

no second chances. Sometimes it's now or never!"

Alan Bennett

JUST DO IT

What has God whispered to you? The first step is to write it all down. Then, look at it, and acknowledge all that is being asked of you. The second step requires that you bring clarity to the whispers. At times, it may be difficult to believe what God has asked of you. For the third step, address your fears.

What do you think holds you back? Detail the obstacles that stand in your way. To receive the fruits of God's grace, you must be able to accept each assignment God places before you. This assignment requires you to apply your faith. It's one thing to hear the call, but it's entirely different when you do nothing about it. Many Christians know the word and pray daily but still find themselves empty inside. Many people have grown up in a church their entire lives.

Others spend time with God consistently; are nice and kind to others, but still have no faith. Application of your faith is one of the hardest lessons to learn in your walk, but it's the only thing that matters. To acquire so much knowledge, but never do anything with it, means nothing in life. When seasons in your life, like the one you're in right now, forces you to stand on faith, you must be ready to apply it.

Every time you stand firmly on the foundation of faith, you strengthen your spirit, and eliminate the power of fear. You no longer turn a cheek to the call, or sweep it under the rug. This means you have, in fact, answered the call. In due time, it will become easier; and you will become victorious. Address the whisper. Give it clarity. Stare fear in the face, and apply your faith. Just do it.

18

LET GOD USE YOU

PHILIPPIANS 2:13

"For it is God who works in you to will and to act in order to fulfill His good purpose."

I received an email from a Pastor that asked if I would be available to speak to his congregation. I so graciously agreed. I didn't waste any time in my reply. I jumped to the call. A few days passed, and I started to question Pastor Randy's request. Did he want me to come to speak for 15 minutes, or did he really want me to speak- like, really speak? I shot him an email to ask for clarification. To my utter shock, Pastor Randy wanted me to deliver the message. He wanted me to preach the word to his entire congregation. I was nervous, scared, and overwhelmed. I didn't have any type of training that I felt qualified me for the task. That's when God reminded me that I am Uniquely Qualified through Him.

"Playing it safe is the riskiest
choice we can ever make."

Sarah Ban Breathnach

Called to Preach

It was confirmed. I would deliver my very first message. I knew God would one day use me through ministry, but I did not think it would be that soon, or to this magnitude. There were so many factors to consider. To state the obvious, I had never preached before. Also, the church was an hour away, and I had never been there. I didn't know the size of the congregation. I didn't know if attendance was in the thousands, or if the church seated 50 people. Plus, I was too scared to ask. Nonetheless, my little fingers quickly typed, "Yes, I will gladly bring the word to your congregation."

For months, I sat in silence and asked God to give clarification on the message He wanted me to deliver. I even called a good friend of mine, David L. to help me out. He reminded me that this was an assignment to be carried out by me, and only me. As much as he wanted to help write my first sermon, he knew I needed to do it alone. His non-help, was the best help I could've received.

Time winded down, and all I had written down in my notes were two paragraphs, on hope and joy. Out of nowhere, the answer I had prayed for fell in my lap, literally. As I went to my Bible for inspiration, an old index card fell out, titled "Hopelessness." This was it! What I had looked for was between the pages of my Bible the entire time. Yet again, God showed His face. He answered my call, in His perfect timing.

Then, the second answer popped up at my doorstep. The week before I was scheduled to preach, I received a DVD in the mail from an old friend. Mark was once a drug dealer and almost went to prison for many years. This was a man who I used to drink and do drugs with. Together, we lived on the wild side.

The DVD was powerful. I watched as he stood before his church to preach his very first message. Mark shared his testimony. Boy, what a powerful story. It was not too different from my own. That's when I clearly heard God tell me, "Let Me use you. Talk about the hopelessness and despair you've felt recently. Share how you found hope. Give your story."

That's exactly what I did. The words flew on the paper so fast. I couldn't stop writing. There was so much power behind my personal testimony. It needed to be shared to bring hope and inspiration to others. People needed to know what I had been through. I needed to share that life hasn't always been easy. Yet, and still, I believed.

The Saturday before I spoke, I sat quietly with my Lord and Savior. I meditated on His word and praised Him. I got a good night's rest. I decided to wake up early to spend time in His perfect peace. I couldn't wait for my brothers to arrive, so we could all travel to the church together, as a family. I was eager to begin my assignment.

Peace Filled

It was my first time in attendance at Greater Faith Missionary Baptist Church, in Hickory, North Carolina. This church was absolutely beautiful. Each person greeted us with open arms. It was "Women's Empowerment Sunday," the entire weekend was dedicated to the celebration of women. My brothers and I joined their Bible study, before service began.

Roughly 100 people sat in the congregation. I walked up to the pulpit and sat in the Pastor's chair. Guess what? I didn't have any nerves. I felt as confident as I did when I delivered that memorable presentation back in high school years ago. The calm smile on my face reflected the peace that had settled in my spirit. I was more so excited, to release the message God had so gracefully placed in my heart. I couldn't wait to get up and share what God had done, through me.

As the choir sang, I profusely thanked the Lord. I was a woman who lacked experience in ministry. I got kicked out of high school and college. I had a criminal record, as a youth and as an adult. I had been arrested for trafficking drugs. I suffered from alcohol abuse. Shoot, I was fired, publicly, from a radio station. How was I about to preach?

I couldn't believe it. God had qualified me. It was by the grace of God I was granted the opportunity to speak and share my journey. Thank You, Lord, thank You Lord, thank You Lord. I stood up and smiled.

I opened the message with a prayer. God unleashed powerful words and stories through me. As I spoke, I watched as the crowd smile back at me in agreement. It was time to look past the words on my paper and solely rely on God. He guided me. He used me. The message was received. What I thought to be light layers of talking points, deeply impacted people's lives. Another one of God's assignments - Completed.

GALATIANS 5:13

"You, my brothers and sisters, were called to be free. But do not use your freedom to indulge the flesh; rather, serve one another humbly."

IT'S NOT EVEN ABOUT YOU

I would call this one of the wisest statements to ever breeze past your ears: "It's not about you, it is about others." We go through life focused on our self, majority of the time. God has equipped us to impact positive change, all around us. It's never about us. Isn't it funny that we actually think it is? We are blessed with spiritual gifts, talents and abilities, solely to help others.

I heard a story from a Pastor about how distraught he was when he learned his daughter was pregnant, out of wedlock. Pastor Andrew was embarrassed and ashamed. He cried to the Lord and asked why it happened to his family. He was confused. He was hurt. He felt that he was a great father.

Therefore, he didn't understand how this had happened to his daughter and his family. He did not know how to stand before his congregation and share this news, but he did it, anyways.

Five years later, he received a call, in the midnight hour,

from a fellow friend and Pastor. His friend, Pastor Jake cried out to him for guidance. He confessed that his son got someone pregnant. He, too, was embarrassed. He was hurt. He was ashamed. He was angry.

As Pastor Andrew drove to his friend's home late one night, he realized everything he had went through five years prior, with his daughter's pregnancy, would help at this very moment. He was able to provide support to his friend. He was able to say, "I got through it, and so can you."

You may not understand why your life takes certain turns, but it's never about you. It's about the people you will meet days, months and even years down the line that need to hear your story. Your story will positively impact their life, forever. Everything you go through in life will prepare you for the next season.

WHO DO YOU REPRESENT?

This activity requires you to look in the mirror and ask yourself, what are you selling? Michelin sells tires. McDonald's sells burgers and fries. Chik-fil-a sells chicken. You would not go to Michelin to buy burgers. That's not what they sell. When you distinctively think of these places, within seconds you know what they sell. They work 24 hours a day, 7 days a week to sell the same things. The same applies for you.

Are you a different person at church, than at work? Are you different at home and with family, than when you are when out in public? If numerous people were asked to describe you, would they all give different descriptions of who you are?

Let the real, genuine, authentic you be free. Sync up who you are, what you do, where you're going, with who you want to be. To do this, you must have the answers to some of these hard questions: Who are you? Why were you created? What's your purpose? Some say, the best moment in life is when you lock in with your purpose.

I used to get scared to post too many pictures of myself on social media. I was fearful that people would think I was narcissistic. There is a thin line that if crossed, it can haunt you forever. Until one day, a gentleman bluntly told me to get from behind the curtain and step into the spotlight. He told me it was time for me to shine, not for myself, but for Jesus. I can openly spam social media, because it's not about me, it's for who I represent- Jesus.

Today, define and conquer the person you are Uniquely

Qualified to be. Become the person who exemplifies peace, joy, and gratefulness. When someone asks, who do you represent, simply answer, "Jesus."

19

THE WARNING

PHILIPPIANS 4:13

"I can do all things through Christ
who strengthens me."

Please understand difficulty will come with this faith journey. Understand, embrace, and respect it. Shout to the mountain top, "Bring it on!" Childbirth is a perfect example. After nine months of ups and downs, the body changes immensely. But, the unbearable pain and turmoil pales in comparison, to the joyous arrival of the newborn baby.

Welcome the challenges that present themselves in any period of life. Respect the process and pay the price. It's only then that you will receive the reward. Storms will rage. Thorns will prick. You have been warned.

FIRST LOSS

As I stepped down from my fulltime career in media,

it was difficult to find a new one. It was crystal clear that God wanted me in ministry, but without much experience, it was hard to land a job. All my experience and degrees were geared toward media. I applied to a few nonprofit jobs, but was turned down, due to the lack of experience. These organizations required at least 10+ years of experience. I had plenty of volunteer experience, but I needed someone to take a chance on me.

Here's when things started to get difficult. I received my first ministry job, and quickly noticed there were payroll issues. After the first couple weeks, I did not receive a check. I was repeatedly promised compensation, but it never came. I held on for five months. I hoped and believed I would get paid at some point, especially, since I loved the work.

For so many years, I had received a salary but was unfulfilled, spiritually. Now, I was fulfilled spiritually, but unable to pay my bills. I was confused. As my savings account dwindled, the bills began to stack up. I eventually had to step down from this role that I loved so much. It saddened me to walk away, but I had to look for a job that could also pay the bills. This taught me that there were two forms of checks to receive. You can receive a paycheck in the form of financial compensation or there's a bigger paycheck, one I like to call, "God's Paycheck".

"God's Paychecks" bring fulfillment to your passion and God-given talents. They bring joy to your heart and it doesn't even feel like work. Some jobs we take on are not about money at all. They're about purpose. The trick is to find a purpose-filled job that supplies "God's Paycheck" and a real paycheck, too.

Had to Eat It

I started to take real estate classes to buy time, as I continued to embark on my path to ministry. I stumbled upon a business deal, which gave me the flexibility to work remotely for a company as an administrative assistant. I enjoyed it, because it allowed me to still take the real estate classes. I learned a lot.

After three months, the company finally finished the first set of projects and received compensation. It had been so long since I had received any income. I anticipated how I would spend the money. I called my boss, eager to pick up my check. There was no answer. I waited for his returned call. After a couple days, I still hadn't heard from him, so I called back.

To my surprise, he had vanished. He never answered his phone, again. He deleted all social media accounts, too. I then decided to Google his name. I wish I would have done that sooner. The very first link warned people not to do business with him. The site displayed his mug shot and cautioned any future business partners of his continued vanishing act, when it came time for him to pay. I had to eat that loss, too.

I am grateful for these experiences of loss. I had to go through these obstacles, to regain my strength for the real world. I no longer worked for a big company, nor was I bound to any contract. I was self-employed. I needed to protect myself. I needed to be smarter with my finances and with whom I conduct business. I had no hard feelings. I immediately forgave the people involved. I also forgave myself for the dumb decisions I had made. I share these experiences with you to warn you. Please understand there will be bumps in the road. Learn from them.

"What you're facing may seem bigger, stronger, or more powerful but don't be intimidated. One touch of God's favor can turn any situation around."

JOEL OSTEEN

KEY PRIORITIES

What are the top priorities in your life? For this activity, let's focus on the top eight most important elements of your life today, in order. What do you fill up on in your life? What do you focus your time and energy on?

List your top eight *key* priorities in your life:

____

____

____

____

____

____

____

____

Before I got saved, my 'top eight' priorities were horrible. I always looked for the next chance to get high. I constantly drank my life away. I focused on men and sex. I enjoyed the rush, as I lived my life on the edge. I partied and pushed the boundaries. I sought attention anywhere I could.

Here were my past top eight priorities:

1. Getting High
2. Drinking
3. Dating
4. Taking Risks
5. Partying
6. Friends
7. Family
8. Education

The only priorities that made any sense were family, friends, and education. However, these were the final three priorities, so they didn't hold much weight at the time. As you can see, my priorities were completely screwed up. As I faced this realization on paper, I learned a lot about myself. First, that God was nowhere to be found. Secondly, there were only two areas listed that could help me become a better person, family and education, that's it! The vast majority of my priorities created more of a hindrance than anything else.

I recommend you create a list of your top eight future priorities. Then compare it to the original list you created earlier. Is there any room for growth? It's very important to examine where you are currently and find areas for improvement. There may also be slight differences in priority level that you want to work on. Take this time to focus on the key priorities in your life.

List the top eight *future* priorities in your life, in order:

____

____

____

____

____

____

____

____

20

MOMENTS OVER MINUTES

PSALMS 46: 10-11

"Be still, and know that I am God."

On your job, you may think you can't slow down, because the person next to you will get the promotion. You may have to juggle two or three hats, to get by. Your job may require you work consistent overtime and holidays. When it comes to being a parent, the idea of slowing down is a joke. There's probably a parent right now trying to go to the bathroom in peace, as the kids bang on the door.

Parents must run the kids to and from school, extracurricular activities, and sports practices. You've heard the saying, "I'll sleep when I'm dead." That's how many people operate, from day to day. They barely grab 4-6 hours of sleep, then wake up to tackle the world, all over again. Who actually has the time to sit down?

Years will begin to pass by, in this constant rat race of life. It's up to you how you spend them. As you speed through 24 hours in a day, don't let life get in the way of your splendor, peace, tranquility, and true happiness. There is something powerful that happens when you are still. Today, drop out of the race. Learn to appreciate life, and all its simplicity.

Sense the Stillness

The first time I captured moments instead of minutes, I immediately became overwhelmed with emotions. I had taken my two little dogs, Lil Reese's and Twix, outside to use the bathroom. Yes, I gave them candy bar names for no particular reason and no, I did not let them wander into any neighbor's yard, just incase you wanted to know. Since I was, and still am an outdoorsy person, I thoroughly enjoyed the frequent trips outside. As I waited on my dogs, I would read, meditate, jot down my thoughts in a journal, eat, and once, even took a nap in my backyard.

One particular day, I took a seat to watch the dogs run around. As they played, I decided to attempt this technique of "being still and in the moment." I closed my eyes and took a deep breath, ready to seize the beauty of the day. The air was warm, and had a nice summertime smell to it. I felt a slight breeze gently dance on my face. The air lightly lifted strands of my hair. It swayed back and forth, and lightly tickled my nose.

The sunshine beamed down directly on me. I looked around and watched the fields of grass move to the call of Mother Nature. I heard the birds happily sing, as they aimlessly flew in the light, blue sky. As I basked in the simplicity of my surroundings, I couldn't help but to smile. I looked at the foundation of my home, and became overjoyed with thankfulness to God. I had been led to that house by Him. Thoughts that had never crossed my mind began to surface.

For instance, how the chair felt as I sat in it; and the feel of the loose, comfortable clothes on my body; and the fact that my dogs were happy and healthy. I had never sat long enough, nor had I paid such close attention to little details like this. Tears rolled down my face, as powerful feelings of gratitude erupted from my spirit. I felt I was unworthy to experience such joy of that magnitude. I was extremely blessed by my surroundings, and was sad for all the times I'd never noticed half of it.

Racing Thoughts

Existence requires work. It is a process and a practice. Learn how to be in the stillness of the moment. This cannot begin with the flip of a switch. Distractions are to blame. Many of us struggle with falling asleep at night, because our minds wander rampantly. A tired body succumbs to a mind that continues to race. We wake up to automatic clouds of thoughts and visions.

We envision the day; what all needs to be done, and wonder whether we completed every task from the day before. Even the trouble of our loved ones run in and out of our thoughts. Each new morning requires a few seconds for us to wrap our minds around our consciousness. Do you wake up to the burdens of reality, or do your first thoughts bask in the gratefulness of life? What do you see before you open your eyes, in the morning?

We go through different scenarios in our heads. So much so, that we cannot see the stories that play out around us. No words have been uttered, but we've already had full blown conversations in our minds. We need to be still. Give ourselves a moment to mentally unwind. Silence the noise.

Your fears may surface as you move to a place of silence, but replace them with thoughts of love and peace. Relive happy moments you experienced as a child. What did it feel like when you fell in love? Think about a time when your grandparent taught you an important lesson, or shared a special story. Relive quiet moments when you sat and rocked your newborn baby to sleep.

Reflect on precious moments you embarked upon as you watched a child fall asleep in your arms. Find whatever mental escape that best mellows your mood. You are rich in love and life. You do not have to chase fulfillment. It already surrounds you. God has showered blessings upon you, at no cost to yourself.

Meditation

To be able to speak to God and hear His word, truly, requires mental cleansing. The purpose of meditation is much deeper than the ability to sit in silence. Deepak Chopra said it best: "Prayer is when you speak to God, but meditation is when God speaks to you." The ability to diminish your thoughts and to hear God's whispers is the art of meditation. It can be difficult to tap into true meditation for the first time. It takes practice.

However, once you feel it for the first time, you will realize that your mind has never slowed down to this pace, ever before. Allow your thoughts to flow into the atmosphere of stillness.

I've struggled with meditation for a long time. In fact, I would fall asleep in the midst of it. I decided to strengthen my spirituality with a 40-day meditation challenge. On day one, I incorporated seven minutes of soothing music. At first, my thoughts ran wild. I found myself in thought about work, what to wear, bills, and if I had returned phone calls. To find a greater focus, I honed in on one thought, and began to have a conversation with it.

Out of nowhere, I felt my body twitch between reality and the attempted meditative state. I would constantly remind myself, "Don't think, meditate!" My first lesson in meditation taught me that I could view my thoughts, but not give them any attention. That took discipline. I learned that when I spent time on any particular thought, that it was not meditation.

Meditation takes time. It is a hard practice to conquer. Do not allow yourself to get frustrated when you cannot relax and quiet your mind. Meditation is a peaceful practice, set to calm you, fully. Simply, push any thought gently out of your mind.

The second day, I sat down to meditate for another seven-minute musical selection. I noticed, when the music stopped that I felt as if I had only sat there for half that time. I was completely surprised. That was a great sign! By the third day, I had extended my meditation session to 15 minutes. I noticed great progress.

Initially, when you begin to meditate, you may notice yourself breathe faster than usual. You will also notice your eyelids jump. Don't be alarmed. Your body is well aware of its unusual state. It is also aware that the journey is still incomplete. The key to meditation is to get in tune with your psyche. When you close your eyes, envision peaceful scenarios, such as sunsets, still waters, and/or nature.

Begin to count backwards from 30 and take slow, deep breaths. Focus your mind and your thoughts on different places of your body. Start from your head, then travel all the way to your feet. Everything will try and steal your attention. The phone rings. A horn blows. The dog barks. A child cries. An alarm goes off. The house makes a squeaky sound. You might even hear the hum of a ceiling fan. The AC comes on. You hear crickets. The mail carrier stops at your mailbox. The trash collector pulls into your cul-de-sac. Stay focused!

Once you get into a deep meditative state, your breathing will become slower and heavier. Your eyelids will no longer pulsate. You will be extremely sensitive to everything around you. You may be able to hear and feel your own heartbeat. You will feel anything that touches your skin. You will fall deep into a trancelike state of silence. Your thoughts will no longer become a concern. You are meditating.

If you haven't attempted meditation, I highly recommend you give it a try. Meditation will strengthen and empower your spiritual growth. It is truly an experience of God's perfect peace.

FIND YOUR PEACE

It's highly important for you to know how to retrieve your peace and tranquility, at any given time. In times of difficulty, when you feel as if you can't go on, you must know how to access God's peace.

Here are a few places I frequent to find my peace. I feel close to God when I'm by the ocean. There is something euphoric, and powerful, yet subtle and gentle, at the same time. I used to go sit at the beach, as a child, and let the wind blow across my face. I imagine the depths of this magnificent ocean God created. I am reminded each time that He is in control.

When I am in nature, I feel close to God because it is He that created all of its beauty. It's the one thing that has not been built and manufactured by us. Jesus' eyes saw trees, dirt, rocks, the sun, and the moon. I feel close to Him in these moments. I feel as if I share the same space as He did 2,000 years ago. I instantly feel at peace in these places. All heaviness leaves, as the smells of the earth overwhelm my senses. I am then able to connect with my truest peace - God.

Now I ask you, where do you find your peace? Is it a massage? Is it through music? Do you find it when you spend time with family? Maybe you find it when you read a book, write in your journal, run, or garden. Recognize what instantly takes you to your place of peace.

20

STOLEN LUNCHES

Philippians 2:13

"For God is working in you, giving you the desire and the power to do what pleases Him."

I walked away from my career, with no idea of what I would do next. I did, however, stand boldly on my love and trust in the Lord. I knew He would carry me through that season. Little did I know, God had led me to my destiny. I began to hear the whispers from the Lord, that I was to start a Bible study. At first, I argued with God about it. I didn't want to waste my time on a hobby. I needed a career. I did not want to devote my time and energy into something that would not bring in an income. I had already learned my lesson. But, God had a plan for my life. He simply looked for a pure heart and an obedient spirit, to carry out His purpose. Then I received this email:

Friendship

God talks so much about friendship in the Bible. That we are divinely designed for it. He says the priority of friendship should be to walk with the wise as iron sharpens iron. We are to find a friend who loves you and has your best interest at heart. The essentials of friendship are to be with someone who influences your life for the better. A true friend leads you to be the best for God. Those friends are hard to find and when you do - we need to spend intentional time and be in contact with them.

As I read these scripture verses...
(Proverbs 13:20, 17:17, 18:24, 27:5-6, Mark 2:1-5)
I can't help but think about you, J! I know that God put us together - even if it was for a short time- to learn from each other. I learned so much from you. You are so wise in your faith and you speak words in truth and love. I just wanted you to know that I miss you so much being in my life every day. You are a gem. A daughter of the King. A very special person and friend. Even though we don't see each other often anymore - I want you to know that you hold a very special place in my heart. You are an amazing woman of God whom I am honored to call friend. I keep you in my thoughts and prayers. I look forward to seeing you soon at yoga and at our lunch date! I just wanted to send you a note of encouragement and love - as you have always done the same for me.

Wishing you a wonderful night and beautiful weekend.

LOTS of LOVE,

KZ

This email from Kristine blessed me, tremendously. It blessed me so much, that I wanted other girlfriends to be blessed, as well. So, I forwarded it. Within a week, I learned they too had shared it with their girlfriends. A ripple effect of love and friendship had taken place. Little did Kristine know, she had answered her assignment with God to plant this seed in my life.

The tugs to start a Bible study grew even stronger. I shared the whispers with my girlfriends. To my surprise, they were overwhelmingly intrigued, and eager to join. Each woman expressed that this was a need in her life. Some shared that this had been a constant prayer for them. They had longed for sisterhood. I set a date.

"If you don't see your worth, you'll always choose people who don't see it either. When your self-esteem rises, your life follows."

MANDY HALE

STOLEN LUNCHES

Kristine agreed to open up her home for the first Bible study. Only we did not know it was an official Bible study yet, we just thought we would gather for girl talk and prayer.

Here was a group of eight women who had extremely busy schedules. We could never make plans with each other, because we all worked opposite shifts. But, God had us steal away from everything, to be in His presence, on that Monday afternoon.

I prayed for God to give me a powerful word, that would speak to the heart of each woman. I did not know where each woman was in her faith journey, nor did I know if everyone even believed in God. I became intimidated by this, but I learned I had to release all the worry and concern to Him. I followed tugs of the Holy Spirit and opened up the session with prayer and scripture. I shared with the ladies that the email on friendship had pierced my heart, and made me want to do more.

As I dove into the lesson, I got so pumped up! I shared that God gave each of us a set of spiritual gifts. I discussed spiritual gifts, gave examples, and definitions, according to the Bible. Then, I decided to go around the room and ask each lady to share what her spiritual gifts were. To my surprise, only Kristine knew her spiritual gifts. No one else knew theirs.

Another woman, went as far as to say, she had prayed to God to reveal what her spiritual gifts were. I immediately felt nervous. We had 30 minutes left in the Bible study, and I did not have a back-up plan. I thought we would use the rest of the session to share with each other. But, if no one had anything to share, what was I supposed to do?

I began to pray. I asked God to intervene and show me what to do. God jumped in and took over. Plan B was formed. We went around the room and had each woman take the "hot seat," so-to-speak. Every woman showered her with praises and shared what they believed her spiritual gifts were.

Within minutes, everyone cried tears of joy. It happened! God showed up in full force. It can be difficult to sit through negative criticism and feedback. But imagine how much more difficult it is to hear someone sing your praises, by the multitude.

A Woman

You are strong
Bold
Lovely
A flower born from a seed
You grew through grace
You stand in elegance
Exude beauty
YOU ARE LOVE

Sometimes you cry
You shout,
You feel hurt
You wild out
You wear all hats
At times, you don't know what to do, but you push forward
YOU ARE LOVE

You are a winner, but have also lost
You stay humble
You are a teacher
You are Uniquely Qualified to walk into your destiny

You have a spiritual calling
A talent only you hold
Your smile is contagious-- show it more often
You create life
You are needed
YOU- DO-IT-ALL

You are wonderfully made
There are no apologies
You are a miracle
God's gift
You are a Blessing to those who know you
Shine brighter, and brighter,
You are a woman
There's nothing in this world like a woman
YOU ARE LOVE

JACINDA JACOBS

Each woman listened intently as everyone shared how she had impacted their lives. The atmosphere began to change. A miraculous transformation took place in all of our hearts. We walked into the house as friends and co-workers, but we left as sisters. We may not have known each other on a personal level. We may not have even spoken on a consistent basis.

But, when God showed up, He tore down all of our walls. Our innermost secrets were exposed. We were fragile and vulnerable. A renewed purpose was established in each of us. God had used me for His good, and it felt wonderful. When women left the Bible study that day, they had tear stained eyes; and felt they'd made an impact in each other's life. All eight women felt valued, important, and loved. They felt that they, in deed, had a place in the world. The one question each woman had as she walked out of the door was, "When do we meet again?"

We decided to call the Bible Studies Stolen Lunches, since we essentially gave up our lunch break to be fed by God. Stolen Lunches Bible Study Community was birthed on August 25th 2014.

From that first Bible study, Stolen Lunches has been a miracle to all of us. It has grown rapidly. We now have Stolen Lunches Bible studies for men. We plan to launch Stolen Lunches Bible studies for kids, in 2017. Our goal is to have Bible studies for the entire family. Our mission, is to intentionally, "Steal away and be fed by God." Women and men now join in from all around the world. What started with just 8 women who decided to give up their lunch break one afternoon, to instead be fed by God, has now blossomed into my calling. It was the answer I was always in search for. An outcry from my heart that I could not see, but with every step, some good and many dark have all led me here.

These small, intimate Bible studies are uniquely orchestrated by God. He has eliminated all answers of "No". A person can never say they're too busy, or not available. This is how I know it's God's design. As we set intentional time to be fed, any person, can join in person or watch and listen live from anywhere in the world.

If you miss it, no worries you can watch or listen to the replay in your free time. In the busyness of life, you can strengthen your faith walk in a unique and technologically savvy way. Our Stolen Lunches Bible Study Community has Bible Studies prayer calls, daily devotionals, mission trips, and an awesome annual "Stolen Weekend" retreat at the beach to wake up before God on the shore at sunrise.

My gift to you, upon reading this book, is not a keychain or a t-shirt, which I would love to create one day, by the way. But, it's an opportunity to increase and strengthen your faith. This is why God created me, to use my media talents for ministry. I build Bible studies so you can be fed by His word. Join a Bible study. I can't wait to meet you- StolenLunches.org.

"Strive to be a positive LIGHT for those
who choose to interact with you."

PEG FITZPATRICK

NOW ASK

MATTHEW 21:22

"All things whatsoever you shall ask in
prayer believing, you shall receive."

Let's dig to the core of your heart's truest desires. God has placed a passion inside of you, that only you can acquire. Now, ask God for it. As the saying goes, "If you don't ask, you won't receive." If you want a new job, ask God for it. You must speak your aspirations into existence. The Bible says write it down and make it plain. Speak it and set a date to obtain it. Believe in it. Understand that God already knows your heart's desire. He put it there for a reason. Be bold. Unlock it and let it free. Do not hesitate to ask God for what you need. My husband always reminds me of James 4:2, "You have not because you ask not." So, don't be afraid, Ask Him.

Write down what you want to ask God:

____

____

____

____

____

____

"You get in life, what you have
the courage to ask for."

OPRAH WINFREY

22

YOU ARE UNIQUELY QUALIFIED

Colossians 1:12

"Giving thanks to the Father, who
has qualified you to share in
the inheritance of the saints in light."

No longer will you live under the reigns of yesterday. You are not fearful; you are not stuck. God created you with a specific destiny in mind. You were created for a beautiful purpose. At times, you may stray away from this path. It's okay. Today is the day you will get back on track. Like a pet that has wandered away from its owner or a car that has veered off the road; You, too, will find your way back to your destiny.

As you gather the strength to endure the day-to-day monotony, believe deep down in your soul that there is a bigger plan for your life. Find gratefulness in your current state. When the time comes to jump, your whole world will change. The only thing constant will be your memory of this moment, right now.

To walk into your destiny, you must first pray. Ask God to intervene. You cannot do it on your own. You need to call on The Most High. Only God can change your circumstances. You may think your situation is impossible, but God can make the impossible situation possible. You are already Qualified.

Make sure you break away from old habits. Just because you were raised a certain way, does not mean you must continue to live that way. Break the cycle. Now is the time to stop. If you continue to do it the same way, you will continue to get the same results. You have the Breastplate of Righteousness, Ephesians 6:14, "To keep your heart pure."

Release yourself of past hurts. This is crucial for you to walk into your destiny. You are not allowed to take any baggage with you. Learn how to release the strongholds. When you hold onto wrongdoings, hurt, anger, and regret, they accumulate and ultimately weigh you down. These ghosts of your past become triggers and can set you off, at any time. Therefore, you must learn to forgive in order to let go. You wear the Belt of Truth, Ephesians 6:14, "To believe in God no matter what worldly circumstances stand in your way."

Be a giver. You show love to others when you give. We may think tangible things, materialistic things, are the only things to give. This is not true. People appreciate love, honesty, and time, among other things. Everyone is in search of love. Guess what? It's free. As you look around your home, you may think you have nothing to give. In actuality, you have so much to offer. Give your heart. Share your wisdom. Show love to a stranger. Give time to loved ones. Take the time to send notes, letters, emails, and texts to let people know you appreciate them.

Become a true giver of the richest, free things in life.

Sit still and listen for God. God's voice is the most beautiful whisper you will ever feel in your spirit. It always comes in His most perfect time. Slow down. If you're too busy, you may miss Him. When God speaks, listen to Him. Most importantly, be obedient. Many times, you already know what God has asked of you. Yet, you may find yourself too scared to move. God's direction will lead you to heavenly peace. He'll continue to whisper and tug at your heart, repeatedly, until you answer.

Fast. Say, "No" to what you want, feel, and need. Say, "Yes" to God. As you continue to live more like Jesus, you must share in His sacrifice and fast. When you fast, it shows The Father that you have surrendered all your ways to Him.

As you begin to propel into a new life - the life you were destined for - there are times you may not feel Qualified. The transition will spark with questions like: "What in the world am I doing?" "Why do I think I can pull this off?" "Will I be able to afford this?" "Will I be able to survive?"

Build a routine of positive, mental chatter. The only person who can stop you from your defined success is you. Your thoughts will make you feel like you're in quicksand, sinking slowly, reaching for a lifeline. The formula is quite simple. Do not allow any negative thoughts to fester for more than a second.

These thoughts will enter your mind, but it's your job to kick them right back out. Keep your mind filled with His Word. Keep your attention on The Most High; slash the darkness with the Sword of the Spirit, Ephesians 6:17, "By standing on the word of God."

As God moves you, shakes you, and changes your life, stay humble and grateful. Gratefulness is the best characteristic to wear on your sleeves, and it's the most beautiful piece of your appearance. Understand that all your plights and your accomplishments are not yours. They are His. Be grateful for His good graces, favor, and direction. In the midst of terrible circumstances, the cure is repeated reflection of gratefulness.

Now, jump! You've asked for it. You've prayed for a change. When God gives you the green light, run toward your destiny like you've been chased by a cheetah. Don't turn back. Don't' slow down. It's time to act. It's time to move. This will be your greatest reward. Be careful what you ask for. When the time comes to jump, be sure you have the guts to do it. When the door opens, are you ready to walk through it?

When God walks you into your destiny, understand that it will require you to be used for His glory. You may find yourself in the strangest places. God wants to use you and take you to new heights. It's not always going to make sense, so take your hands off the wheel and let Him drive. Be a vessel for God, and let Him use you. The realization in your heart that God has orchestrated makes it all worth it. You will walk in the Gospel of Peace, Ephesians 6:15, "Knowing that in the midst of the storm you stand protected by God."

As you walk into your destiny, you will learn that this whole process, ultimately, has nothing to do with you. Your destiny involves saving someone else's life. There's a little girl, or a little boy who, perhaps, in five years will come cross your path. Will you be ready to change their life? Will you be able to share your story of how you endured the storm? Will you be able to share hope, faith, and ultimate peace?

The warning is raw and real. This is not an easy feat. The battle is long, treacherous, and scary. It will require sweat. It will require tears. God picks ordinary people to do extraordinary things, in His Name. The only thing He looks for is a pure heart. As you answer the call, darkness will chase after you and scream, "Leaving so soon?" You will be tested. You will be challenged. At times, you may feel you have made the wrong decision. But God has given you the armor of protection and the weapons, to defeat. Your battle is already won. God has your back. Trust and believe. You are protected by the Shield of Faith, Ephesians 6:16, "Knowing that God is a God of His Word."

Remember to stay in the moment. As life begins to move around you, take the time to be still and bask in His presence. Do not get caught up in the hurried pace of life. The best moments in life are when you can enjoy your current moment. Remember to make intentional time to spend with God. When times get hard, lean on God for every area of your life.

When He begins to bless your life, don't get so consumed that you forget to spend time with Him. Take the time now to notice the many blessings all around you. Never take for granted the favor He showers upon you, daily. From head to toe, you have the Helmet of Salvation, Ephesians 6:17, "To keep your thoughts focused on God."

I pray this book has given you hope. I wanted you to know that you're not alone. I have walked the same road with you. Some minor details may be different; the overall theme is our heart craves for more. When the time is right, God will give you the thumbs up. Run full speed toward the edge of the cliff. When you look around, you will see people stare at you, laugh and point, but pay them no mind.

Run toward your freedom. Run to your destiny. When you take that last step, jump as far as you can. You will find yourself in midair, with your arms held high in the sky. You are flying, free-falling into your new life. A life of purpose. A life of expectancy. A life of worth. A life of substance.

This is a feeling you can only dream of. But, God has it in your future. Believe in Him. Trust in Him. There is no better feeling in the world than to walk into your purpose. To grab hold of your destiny. The one He designed, perfectly for you.

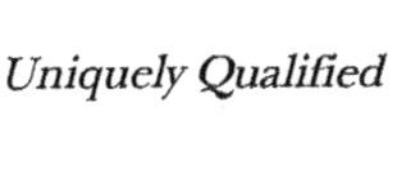

You are *Uniquely Qualified* to walk into your destiny.

SINCERELY GOD, THANK YOU

God, I thank You for my husband, Derrick Jacobs. I am thankful that You created and developed every part of him. God, I know You created us perfectly for one another. I thank You for the gift of friendship, service of love, and smiles of laughter. I thank You for the instant connection of our spirits. We understand our call and are ready to impact the world for You. I thank You for his strength, his hustle, talents, and ability to make anything I need happen. Thank You for showing me the perfect love of a man. God, thank You for making me fit to receive his love.

God, I thank You, for my family. I thank You for my sweet, sweet mother, who gives until there's nothing left. Her love flows like a river. Her love encompasses all that I am. When I hit the lowest of the low, she was the only one there to pick me up. She never judged me. She always knew I would do great things, even when I was at my worst.

Thank You, God, for blessing me with this little lady. Her spiritual gifts overflow into me, and I am so blessed. I pray the words in this book will speak to her heart and change her life, to bring her closer to You. Thank you for answered prayers as my mom accepted Christ as her Lord and Savior on November 20, 2016.

Thank You, God, for my brother Landon. We were so close growing up. I remember dressing him up like a girl, because I wanted him to be a sister. I got in a lot of trouble for that! Thank You for giving me Landon to grow up with. God, thank You, for all the trials and tribulations we had. For two years, we did not speak. Thank You, for the trip to Barbados, when we picked up right where we left off.

Thank You, for his move to Charlotte, and for his new beginning. Thank You, for the day You answered my prayers, and he got saved. Thank You, for Your work in him. God, he tries every day to break the chains and I thank You. God, if it wasn't for him, I would certainly be dead today. The crazy life I lived had a stopping point, because I knew he was watching. Thank You, for showing me how much of an influence I am to him. Thank You, God, for speaking to him daily and guiding his hand.

God, thank You, for my brother Jaris. From a young age, my brother walked to the beat of his own song. I thought it was weakness, but now I learned that he was the smarter one out of all of us. Thank You, God, for him. He taught me that you have to make decisions in life based on where you are and where you're going, not based on what others are doing. Success is defined in one's self not on how others perceive you. He taught me to accept and love my authentic self. Thank You, God.

No matter how he feels or what he thinks, my brother chooses to love, because that is Your desire in Heaven. This is a tough characteristic to hold, but he wears it proudly. I am always his audience. We share something so special. God, I thank You for him. I have loved every moment of growing up with him.

For my father, God, I thank You. You taught me everything I needed in life at a very young age. My strong will and ability to not put up with anything less than the best is all from you. Lord, I am extremely grateful for every time we get to speak on the phone- Thank you God, for answered prayers. I know after our family broke up, we all suffered and endured a lot of pain.

My God's voice never wavered as He whispered, continuously, "Never give up on your dad." I will never forget, just as I was about to walk down the aisle, then the elevator door swung open and there you were. A dream I had since a child, for my dad to walk me down the aisle. Thank you! It's moments like this, that let me know God is real and that He had always heard my cry. Me, Landon and Jaris love you unconditionally.

God, I thank You for my one special friend, Adrienne. We talk every day. She has been my greatest friend since the 5th grade, at Aberdeen Elementary School, in Hampton, Virginia. She wore those thick, pink glasses, but she was my friend, almost instantaneously. Today, we are still glued to the hip, with distance never being a factor. I thank God, for our friendship.

For the intentional time spent during the highs and lows. I thank You for instilling such patience and understanding in her. I thank you for showing her how to love all my flaws and to never judge. I thank you for teaching us to be a "we."

My prayer for her today is to experience a deeper walk with you. I pray she grabs hold of Your hand.

I think of all my friends I have met and chilled with along the way. The state of Virginia raised me and Charlotte, North Carolina has become my home. I thank God for each person I have encountered from school, church, to work. I thank those who have planted seeds in my life. Thank you for the deep conversation. Thank you for loving me.

To my Lisa, thank you for falling in love with me and taking me into your family. When I was all alone, you raised me up. To Susan, thank you for speaking life over me every time you see me. To Romona, my guardian angel, thank you for answering the call every time God speaks to you.

To all the friends who helped shape me and mold me, thank you for the life lessons. Thank you for showing me how to love and how to receive love.

For all the different employment arenas that have given me an opportunity, even when I didn't have an ounce of talent- thank You, God.

For Tyler who helped me edit this book when it was "hot" mess, I thank you. For Jean, thank you for our late-night sessions, friendship, servanthood and obedience in pushing me to complete God's assignment, and as you say, "Set the captives free."

For everyone who prayed over this book and pushed me, motivated me, supported me through this process- I can't thank you enough. This has been one of the hardest journeys to endure, but today, it's all worth it. For those of you who are reading this, thank you. I pray that you have been blessed by Uniquely Qualified.

Coming soon . . .
Uniquely Qualified
Volume II

ABOUT THE AUTHOR

Jacinda Jacobs is a motivational speaker in Charlotte, North Carolina. With over 15 years in the media business. She started her career in radio as an on-air morning personality and later, transitioned into television news. For multiple seasons she has graced fans with her high energy and loving personality as an arena host for the NBA's Charlotte Hornets. She learned however, that there must purpose to the mic for her to sustain peace within, and to fulfill her calling.

Jacinda and her husband run a global Bible study organization called, Stolen Lunches Bible Study Community, set to inspire and empower people of all ages to strengthen their faith walk. She is married to her best friend and co-host, Derrick "FlyTy" Jacobs. She is a bonus mom to three amazing boys and they have three loud dogs. She is excited to wake up each morning, and live out the purpose God has over her life. For more, log onto IamUniquelyQualified.com and MsJacinda.com.